T0300878

Effectiveness of Anti-Corruption Agencies in East Africa

Kenya, Tanzania and Uganda

A review by AfriMAP

December 2015

Published by African Minds on behalf of
Open Society Foundations
224 West 57th Street
New York, NY 10019
www.opensocietyfoundations.org

African Minds
4 Eccleston Place, Somerset West, 7130, Cape Town, South Africa
info@africanminds.org.za
www.africanminds.org.za

ISBNs
978-1-928331-14-8 Print
978-1-928331-15-5 e-Book
978-1-928331-16-2 e-Pub

Copies of this book are available for free download at www.africanminds.org.za

ORDERS
To order printed copies from Africa, please contact:
African Minds
Email: info@africanminds.org.za
To order printed copies from outside Africa, please contact:
African Books Collective
PO Box 721, Oxford OX1 9EN, UK
Email: orders@africanbookscollective.com

Contents

Preface

Corruption has a detrimental impact on the development of any country, for it affects the effective provision of public services, particularly services to the most vulnerable groups in society. Despite the plethora of efforts deployed to combat corruption, it remains an endemic problem in most countries of sub-Saharan Africa. East Africa is no exception. According to Transparency International's Corruption Perception Index for the year 2014, out of the 175 countries and territories studied, rankings for Tanzania (119th), Kenya (145th), and Uganda (142nd) remained low. Needless to say, high-profile corruption cases have come to light in all countries under study. Some have been channelled through the proper authorities, and outcomes and findings have been made public. But most are still pending, have simply been smothered by executive orders, or have become entangled in convoluted political processes that seem never-ending. However, efforts have been made at the national, regional, continental and international levels to establish institutions to combat corruption, and anti-corruption laws have been passed. The African Union Convention on Preventing and Combating Corruption defines a series of corruption-linked offences in article 4, and article 5 on 'the legislative and other measures' requires member states to 'establish, maintain and strengthen independent national anti-corruption authorities or agencies'. Other measures include the strengthening of internal accounting and auditing systems, in particular in the public sector, the protection of witnesses and informers in corruption cases, denouncing corruption-promoting systems, and educating the populations on corruption. In another provision, the AU Convention sets out that 'the national Authorities or Agencies' responsible for combating corruption related offences 'enjoy the necessary independence and autonomy enabling them to carry out their duties effectively' (article 20(4)). The current East African Community (EAC) Protocol on Preventing and Combating Corruption is only in draft form. But its current draft does not mention anti- corruption commissions specifically in the text. However, article 6 (b) does compel the partner states to adopt measures and strategies to strengthen institutions responsible for enforcing mechanisms for preventing and detecting, as well as watchdog and good-governance institutions. It further states that 'the competent authorities shall be vested with prosecutorial powers for the purposes of implementing this protocol'. The scope of the instrument covers the following:

- Preventive measures;
- Enforcement;
- Asset recovery and forfeiture;
- Regional cooperation; and
- Technical assistance

A large number of East African countries had enacted anti-corruption laws and had established agencies devoted to helping control corruption even before the adoption of the AU Convention.

Nonetheless, there is still strong scepticism within the East Africa region regarding the effectiveness of these institutions, which are vigorously criticised in view of the disparity that exists between the governments' anti-corruption rhetoric and the impunity enjoyed by public servants. One can hardly state with certainty that the emergence of these agencies will give rise to a genuine decline in corruption. At times, one is inclined to suspect that these agencies do not enjoy sufficient independence to enable them to fulfil their mandate effectively. The real autonomy of these agencies vis-à-vis the executive should be examined, and, likewise, their broad mandate, which affords them powers to institute legal proceedings, as well as the need to provide them with sufficient resources to deal with the magnitude and significance of systemic corruption. One is therefore left wondering whether the numerous anti-corruption agencies have only been put in place to appease international donors and whether their actual objective is to find durable solutions to the corruption problem – or are they simply a façade of an institution that is undermined and is ill-equipped to address grand corruption. This analysis is justified, in that several countries which are highly dependent on aid and which are bound by the anti-corruption requirements often included in the key conditions attached to this aid may have been tempted to take this easy way out. Studies carried out with regard to anti-corruption agencies around the world have established reasons to justify the failings of some of them. Among these are: lack of political will; absence of a national global strategy; inadequate legal frameworks and insufficient or inappropriate resources; limited autonomy and low public confidence; the lack of an enabling climate and the necessary know-how; the isolation of some agencies; and the lack of integrity. Efforts were made to verify these conclusions in relation to the agencies under consideration in the present study. In the final analysis, continuing efforts are needed to reach a collective agreement as to whether, in fact, anti-corruption agencies in Africa, and particularly the EAC, constitute effective tools for combating corruption, or whether greater efforts and investments are needed to enhance the criminal justice system, accounting and banking standards, or other measures, beyond just political will and effective leadership.

Ozias Tungwarara
Research Manager
Africa Regional Office

Methodology

As far back as 2011, discussions were ongoing within AfriMAP and among its partners and within the Open Society Foundations in Africa as regards the viability of conducting a study on the effectiveness of anti-corruption commissions in Africa. The idea was to undertake a comparative study which would examine the rationale underlying the successes and failures of agencies or mechanisms devoted to the prevention and combating of corruption in East African countries, with the aim ultimately being to establish ways and means of strengthening anti-corruption efforts on the African continent.

Accordingly, in the present study, and in the context of the general, legal anti-corruption framework in each of the countries under discussion, the various agencies' responsibilities are assessed together with their status and that of its members. Forming part of such assessment are these agencies relations with the general public and other stakeholders, as well as their overall performance and impact. Such assessment has culminated in a set of recommendations identified in the present study, as well as in solutions to issues such as the relevance of the anti-corruption institutions and the necessary roles, measures and conditions required for their effective operationalisation.

In the final analysis, the researchers examined whether in fact the agencies constitute effective tools for combating corruption, or whether greater effort and investment are called for in order to enhance the criminal justice system, accounting and banking standards, or other measures. The study was complemented by a series of desk reviews, by focused group discussions, and by interviews with critical stakeholders, policymakers, CSOs, and lawmakers at the national level. All the country reports were subjected to rigorous in-country validations, where senior staff members of the respective anti-corruption commissions were represented so as to ensure that the information and data presented in the draft reports were accurate. The reports were also subjected to peer reviews.

About the contributors

Kenya: Job Ogonda is a development executive with over 18 years' experience in leading national and regional institutions and programmes. He has over 16 years' leadership experience, providing institutional, knowledge and project leadership at Transparency International, the United Nations, the International Centre for Development, and HelpAge International. He is currently an extractives sector advisor to the Ministry of Mining (Kenya Government), advisor to the government of South Africa on accountability in the public service, governance consultant to the East African Community, accountability advisor to Adam Smith International, and governance advisor to the Institute for Human Rights and Business. He was previously an Africa regional advisor on public administration and anti-corruption with the UNDP-Africa Regional Office in Addis Ababa. He sits on the boards of the National Democratic institute (NDI) and the Institute of Ethics-East Africa, and previously sat on the board of the Institute of Directors (IoD).

His areas of specialisation include governance (with emphasis on accountability, economic governance, and public administration and performance), social development, and economic development. Job Ogonda holds a master's degree in development and a bachelor's degree in economics.

The first drafts of the Kenya chapter were authored by Mwalimu Mati, who is the co-founder of an internet web portal dedicated to exposing, documenting and indexing information on corruption in Kenya.

Tanzania: Moses Kulaba is currently the founding executive director of the Governance and Economic Policy Centre (GEPC), a not-for-profit organisation based in Dar es Salaam, Tanzania. Previously, he was executive director of Agenda Participation 2000 (AP2000) and was responsible for establishing the Tanzania Corruption Tracker System, an online portal for documenting corruption cases in Tanzania. He has an extensive training background in political science, development management and law, and has over 13 years' experience in governance, democratisation, and public-policy analysis. He has conducted and participated in various studies and projects for leading agencies like Policy Forum, the UNDP, the EU, the DFID, Concern, OSIEA and the International Budget Project (IBP) and has written extensively in the areas of corruption, illicit capital flight, and development. His current interests are natural-resources governance, petroleum policy and resources management, and taxation.

Uganda: Dan Ngabirano is an assistant lecturer in the School of Law, Makerere University, in Kampala, Uganda. He is also a consulting partner at Development Law Associates (DLA), a legal consultancy firm with a keen interest in law and development across the African continent. Over the years, Dan's work has focused on: anti-corruption law and practice; the right to information; transparency and accountability; and natural-resources governance. He previously worked and consulted for a number of organisations including: the Open Society Initiative for East Africa (OSIEA), Open Society Foundations, Carter Centre, Global Integrity, World Resources Institute (WRI), Article 19, Advocates Coalition on Development and Environment (ACODE), Avocats San Frontieres, Human Rights Network Uganda (HURINET-U), Kitua Cha Katiba (KCK), Greenwatch Uganda, Africa Freedom of Information Centre (AFIC), and the International Law Institute (ILI), among others.

Dan holds a master of laws (LLM) degree from Harvard University in the United States of America, Bachelor of Laws degree (LLB) from Makerere University, and a Postgraduate Diploma in Legal Practice from the Law Development Centre (DLA). He has been admitted to practise law in Uganda and is an active member of the Uganda Law Society and the East African Law Society. He is also a member of several groups that promote transparency and accountability. Some of these include the Access Initiative (TAI) and the Access to Information Committee of the African Network of Constitutional Lawyers (ANCL).

Acknowledgements

This first volume on assessing the effectiveness of anti-corruption agencies, which covers Kenya, Tanzania and Uganda, was made possible by contributions and the participation of the following persons, for which they are sincerely thanked: Agnes Hanti, Programme Officer, Open Society Initiative for Eastern Africa (OSIEA) Tanzania Programme; Adam Anthony, Programme Assistant, OSIEA Tanzania Programme; Magdalene Kioko, Programme Manager, OSIEA Kenya Programme; Mary W Gathegu, Programme Assistant OSIEA Kenya Programme; Richard Mugisha, Programme Officer, OSIEA Uganda Programme; Rita Nalumansi, Programme Assistant OSIEA Uganda Programme; Josephine Ihuthia, Programme Assistant, OSF's Africa Regional Office (AFRO); Maureen Kimatu, Executive Assistant, OSIEA Director's Office; and Chris Abuor, Intern OSIEA Kenya Programme.

Appreciation is expressed to the Africa Foundation's Regional Office's (AfRO) Anti-Corruption Cluster members: Pascal Kambale, Ibrahima Kane, Yaye Helene Ndiaye, Thandi Mosala and Sarah Pray for the strategic support they contributed to the project. Jeggan Grey-Johnson, Programme Officer, AFRO, led the work of the cluster, edited all the chapters, and facilitated the country validation meetings.

The regional editor, Job Ogonda, showed total dedication in his role, thereby adding much value to the final publication.

1

Overview

A. Executive summary

Corruption in the three East African countries' public sector remains endemic. Whilst the media and civil society have for at least a decade freely exposed corruption scandals, the exposure has not ended corruption and its attendant impunity. The laws and institutions to combat corruption are in place and yet the situation does not seem to improve.

In all three countries, there is a clear correlation between the levels of campaign financing and the profit motive for accessing public office. A report by Cambridge University[1] found that illegal funds were used to finance the Kenya African National Union's elections in the 1990s. The funds were raised through the so-called Goldenberg affair, whereas those aimed at financing the National Rainbow Coalition's elections in December 2007 were to be raised through what became known as the Anglo Leasing scandal. A 2005 report by the National Democratic Institute (NDI) on electioneering in Tanzania noted that respondents decried the domination of wealthy individuals who seek office in order to gain access to and control over lucrative contracts, and business contributors who demand paybacks from those whom they support politically. As a result, the political establishment is often seen as a circle of wealthy individuals who make policy decisions based on private interests, rather than the common good.

Kenya, Uganda and Tanzania have all ratified the United Nations Convention against Corruption (UNCAC) and the African Union Convention on Preventing and Combating Corruption (AU Convention). In addition, all three have passed laws to domesticate these conventions to a large degree.

The three national anti-corruption agencies examined in this report are reported to

---

1   See: http://journals.cambridge.org/actiondisplayAbstract?fromPage=online&aid=1874776&fileId=S0022278X 08003224.

be ineffective against grand corruption or corruption connected to politically powerful individuals and entities. Kenya's Ethics and Anti-Corruption Commission (EACC) has consistently been destabilised, or has been under threat of destabilisation, since its inception. It is strange that most instances of destabilisation seem to coincide with periods when progress is being made on 'politically sensitive cases'.

The three national anti-corruption agencies independently appoint their heads through a process of open competition. They also enjoy relative autonomy under their respective laws.

The staff of these agencies are appointed through competitive, open processes and are given limited-period contracts, which are renewable. The agencies have also devolved to a limited extent beyond their respective national headquarters.

They all have clear mandates to prevent corruption and to sensitise and educate the public in the fight against corruption. Despite this, they are not well regarded by the public, most of whom claim not to report corruption to these agencies out of a belief that nothing will happen. Whilst all three agencies have had relative success in pursuing bureaucratic corruption, none has had any successful prosecutions involving grand corruption.

The agencies in Kenya and Tanzania do not have prosecutorial powers, but Uganda's agency does. Prosecutorial power in Kenya and Tanzania is vested in the directorates of public prosecutions.

All three agencies face the challenge of inadequate resources, mainly due to government resource constraints.

The individual country reviews in this report broadly recommend that the anti-corruption agencies establish a presence in all areas of their respective countries in order to better serve the population. They further recommend that the agencies in Kenya and Tanzania be given powers to prosecute alleged perpetrators. The reports also recommend the adequate allocation of resources to the agencies.

B. State of corruption

The state of corruption in the three countries has deteriorated since the advent of Transparency International's (TI) East African Bribery Index, as indicated in Table 1.1.

Table 1.1: Incidence of bribery in Kenya, Uganda and Tanzania, 2009 and 2014

Country	Bribery incidence (%) 2009	Bribery incidence (%) 2014
Kenya	45	41
Uganda	35	43
Tanzania	17	48

The reports attribute the high prevalence of corruption and its increasing incidence to the lack of political will to fight this scourge. This is, in turn, attributed, in part, to the capture of the state through political processes, especially elections, by business, the ruling party and certain individuals.

C. Civil society, donors and media engagement

All three national agencies communicate with the public and have partnerships with government departments, semi-autonomous government agencies, as well as state corporations.

Kenya, Tanzania and Uganda all have well-developed and independent media that have consistently reported on corruption and advocated for accountability and transparency in the use of public resources.

The donor community has been vocal against the levels of corruption in the respective three countries since the early 1990s. The Tanzanian and Ugandan agencies have received donor funding since their inception, and continue to do so. Kenya's EACC received no donor funding in 2014, despite significant funding gaps. This is an astounding decline from USD1.26 million (15% of annual expenditure) in 2011.

The three countries all have robust civil societies that have consistently agitated for accountability and transparency. Over the last five years, however, there has been increased repression of civil-society groupings through legal measures as well as physical intimidation.

D. Commitment to international conventions on corruption

Kenya, Uganda and Tanzania have all ratified the UNCAC and the AU Convention. The respective agencies are members of the East African Association of Anti-Corruption Authorities (EAAACA).[2] The three countries have also passed laws to domesticate the UN and AU conventions.

E. Legal frameworks for preventing and combating corruption

Kenya, Tanzania and Uganda have extensive legal frameworks that could, if effectively implemented, significantly reduce corruption. These include laws that:

- Establish the anti-corruption agencies, their functioning, independence and oversight;
- Provide for the regulation, management, expenditure and accountability of election-campaign funds during elections;
- Enforce standards of ethics and integrity among public officers;
- Provide for the criminalisation of money laundering and the establishment of an independent institution responsible for combating money laundering;
- Provide for the protection, rights and welfare of victims of offences; and
- Provide for the right to access public information.

---

2   For more information about the EAAACA, go to its website at http://eaaaca.org/?page_id=16.

F. Anti-corruption agencies

The three countries' anti-corruption agencies have evolved from the law-enforcement units established during colonial times. Their characteristics and status can be summarised as in Table 1.2.

Table 1.2: The status and characteristics of the Ugandan, Kenyan and Tanzanian anti-corruption agencies

Status/ characteristic	Uganda **Inspector General of Government**	Kenya **Ethics and Anti-Corruption Commission (EACC)**	Tanzania **Prevention and Combating of Corruption Bureau (PCCB)**
Constitutional anchoring and independence	Established by the Constitution and an Act of parliament. Reports to parliament	Established by the Constitution and an Act of parliament. Reports to parliament	Not anchored in the Constitution, but established by an Act of parliament in 2007. It also reports to the presidency, not parliament, and is therefore not perceived to be independent
Stability	Has been relatively stable	Has been disbanded, or seriously disrupted, at least nine times since its inception in 1997	Has been relatively stable
Governance	Has an oversight board consisting of the inspector general (IG) as its chairperson, two deputy IGs, the secretary, the chairperson of the Public Service Commission, the Minister of Public Service and two members appointed by the president	Has a commission that oversees the performance of the secretariat staff	Has no oversight mechanism that is independent of the executive and parliament
Capacity	Has staff in 16 parts of Uganda	Has 264 staff distributed over five regions who are competitively recruited, and trained in key functions	Has 2 086 staff distributed all over the country who are competitively recruited and trained in key functions.
Security of tenure	IG and two deputy IGs enjoy security of tenure after appointment for a four-year renewable term	Five part-time commissioners have security of tenure after appointment for a single term of five years. Staff have renewable contracts	Director general does not have specified security of tenure. Staff have renewable contracts
Ethics		Code of ethics exists for commissioners and staff and is enforced	Code of ethics exists for staff and is enforced

Status/ characteristic	Uganda Inspector General of Government	Kenya Ethics and Anti-Corruption Commission (EACC)	Tanzania Prevention and Combating of Corruption Bureau (PCCB)
Remuneration	The IG opined that their salary levels should at least be at the same levels as those of employees in the Office of the Auditor General	Generous by global standards. Ranges from USD8 500 to USD800	Generous, relative to public-service levels
Investigative and prosecutorial powers	Has investigative and prosecutorial powers	Has investigative but no prosecutorial powers	Has investigative but no prosecutorial powers. Mandate is limited to the mainland and does not extend to Zanzibar
Public-feedback mechanism	Complainants are given a code through which they can track the complaint. They also receive feedback both orally and in writing at the closing of the complaint	After submitting a report, the public can create an anonymous postbox from where to access feedback	There is no set feedback mechanism
Witness protection	None	There is a witness protection law that is yet to be operationalised.	None
Financing	IG bids, along with other independent bodies and ministries, for annual budgetary allocations awarded by parliament in the national budget. Such allocations are currently deemed inadequate	The commission bids, along with other independent bodies and ministries, for annual budgetary allocations awarded by parliament in the national budget. Such allocations are currently deemed inadequate	Submits budget to minister responsible for good governance for tabling in parliament
Performance	In 2013, the IG received 1 513 complaints, investigated 254, and instituted 83 prosecutions which led to three convictions	In 2014, the Commission received 3 355 complaints, investigated and forwarded 1 688, 32 dockets for prosecution, of which 28 were approved	In 2013, the Bureau received 5 456 complaints, investigated and forwarded 1 100, 354 dockets forwarded for prosecution, of which 343 were approved

G. Conclusion

Corruption in the three countries remains a significant challenge. While sound legal frameworks for fighting corruption exist, there seem to be deliberate efforts by the executives and parliaments in the respective countries to limit or defeat the abilities of anti-corruption agencies to do their job. This manifests itself through changes in some laws and a failure to act according to others, as well as in intimidation and the constraining of budgets.

The following country reports make far-reaching recommendations on how legal and institutional reforms can make each agency more effective.

2

Kenya

A. Executive summary

Corruption remains endemic to Kenya's public sector. The media and civil society have, for at least a decade, freely exposed corruption scandals; however, this exposure has not ended corruption and its attendant impunity. The laws and institutions to combat corruption are in place and yet the situation does not improve.

Prevention, suppression and punishment of corruption frequently feature in Kenyan political rhetoric, but rarely is this rhetoric matched by action. Kenya has seen consistent promises and then attendant inaction concerning corruption since independence. Analysts note that the levels of campaign financing indicate that the race for political office is partly motivated by profit. A report by Cambridge University found that illegal funds were used to finance the Kenya African National Union's elections in the 1990s.[3] The funds were raised through the so-called Goldenberg affair, whereas those aimed at financing the National Rainbow Coalition's elections in December 2007 were to be raised through what was known as the Anglo Leasing scandal.

Kenya ratified the United Nations Convention against Corruption (UNCAC) on 9 December 2003. On 3 February 2007, Kenya ratified the African Union Convention on Preventing and Combating Corruption (AU Convention). Kenya is a partner state and has expressed support for the draft East African Community Protocol on Preventing and Combating Corruption. The Ethics and Anti-Corruption Commission (EACC) is a founding member of the East African Association of Anti-Corruption Authorities (EAAACA). As of July 2014, Kenya's national assembly had passed laws to domesticate the UNCAC and AU conventions, including the 2012 Leadership and Integrity Act, the

---

3   See: http://journals.cambridge.org/action/displayAbstract?fromPage=online&aid=1874776&fileId=S0022278
     X08003224.

2011 Ethics and Anti-Corruption Commission Act, and the 2009 Proceeds of Crime and Anti-Money Laundering Act.

The EACC was established under article 79 of the Constitution of 2010. The EACC has consistently been the target of major destabilisation, or the threat of destabilisation, since its inception. It is strange that most instances of destabilisation seem to coincide with periods when the institution seems to be making progress on politically sensitive cases.

The commission appoints, with the approval of the national assembly, a suitably qualified person to be the commission secretary. The commission secretary is the commission's chief executive officer, as well as its accounting officer.

The commissioners of the EACC are state officers as per the Constitution. Commission staff are appointed through competitive, open processes and are given limited-period contracts that are renewable. The commissioners of the EACC have security of tenure through certain constitutional guarantees. The EACC has its headquarters in Nairobi, Kenya's capital, and has five regional offices in major towns (Mombasa, Kisumu, Nyeri, Eldoret and Garissa).

The EACC has a clear mandate in terms of the prevention of corruption, as well as regarding the sensitisation and education of the public in the fight against corruption. However, the EACC is not widely relied upon by Kenyans in reporting corruption. For example, a 2012 survey by the commission found that, whereas 60% of those surveyed had 'observed or witnessed a corrupt act by a public officer' in the past 12 months, only 6% reported the incident. The EACC has a public-feedback mechanism whereby, after submitting a report, a member of the public has the option of creating an anonymous postbox in order to receive feedback on progress in handling the issue. It operates a German-designed, online whistle-blowing system known as the Business Keeper Management System (BKMS), sponsored by GIZ, which facilitates anonymous online corruption reporting. The EACC and its predecessors have seen some successes. It has investigated over 13 000 cases and successfully developed over 650 cases for prosecution between 2008 and 2013. The commission also recovered KES6.8 billion (USD80.4 million) during the same period.

The commission does not have prosecutorial powers. Such power is vested in the Director of Public Prosecutions.

The EACC perennially faces the challenge of inadequate resources, as it is not allocated its annual budget request. This is mainly due to government resource constraints.

This report recommends the reinstatement of a previous governance structure that separated the secretariat, with its technical and implementation responsibility, and an oversight board that held the secretariat to account. The report also recommends that the EACC establish a presence in each county if it is to adequately meet the expectations and needs of the majority of the population. It further recommends that the EACC be given powers to prosecute.

The report further recommends adequate allocation of resources to enable the EACC to execute its mandated functions. In 2014, the EACC reported no partnerships with donors or non-governmental organisations (NGOs). Also worth noting is the fact that the EACC received no donor funding despite significant funding gaps. This is an astounding decline from KES126 million (15% of annual expenditure) in 2011.

B. Introduction

Since the late 1990s, anti-corruption has been a major policy issue in Kenya. The government initially perceived the raising of the issue as simply a matter of foreign-donor intervention, though it later gradually began to address the issue. Despite this, corruption in Kenya's public sector remains endemic. Practised with impunity, Kenyan corruption is also much studied and recorded. Citizens report bribery experiences with great frequency. Moreover, the and civil society have, for at least a decade, freely exposed corruption scandals, and, in truth, operate in an environment that is not as oppressive as, the first three decades of independence. This exposure has not, however, ended corruption. The laws and institutions to combat corruption are in place and yet the situation does not improve.

This report looks at the Kenyan EACC and attempts to assess the reasons for its successes and failures as an anti-corruption body. The EACC was established pursuant to the Constitution of 2010 as an investigative body without prosecutorial powers. Its statutory bases and structures are described in detail below and some key developmental events in its history and activities are analysed. The chapter ends with some policy conclusions and recommendations.

C. State of corruption

Despite its domination of political-competition rhetoric, and despite regime change, corruption in Kenya's public sector remains endemic. Citizens report bribery experiences with great frequency. An NGO[4] contains records of citizens' complaints about official bribery demands. Following the advent of multiparty democracy in 1992, media and civil society have frequently exposed corruption scandals in an environment that is less repressive, yet where corruption continues with impunity.

In the decade since 2003, Kenya's score on Transparency International's Corruption Perceptions Index (CPI) has never been higher than 3/10. According to the CPI, this indicates that corruption in Kenya's public sector is perceived to be rampant by survey respondents. Table 2.1 records Kenya's ranking on the CPI from 2002 to 2013.

An empirical survey tool developed in 2001 by the Kenya chapter of Transparency International documents bribery experiences of Kenyans in their interactions with Kenyan public institutions. Each year, the Kenya Bribery Index (KBI) observes that Kenyans frequently have corruption experiences in their interactions with national and local government institutions. The lawenforcement sector and the police, in particular, are ranked as the most corrupt Kenyan institution in all editions of the KBI.

---

4   http://ipaidabribe.or.ke

Table 2.1: Kenya score and rankings in the CPI (2002–2013)

Year	CPI score	Ranking/no. of countries ranked	No. of surveys used to compile CPI
2002	1.9	96 / 102	5
2003	1.9	122 / 133	7
2004	2.1	129 / 145	7
2005	2.1	144 /158	8
2006	2.2	142 / 163	7
2007	2.1	150 / 179	8
2008	2.1	147 / 180	7
2009	2.2	146 / 180	7
2010	2.1	154 / 178	7
2011	2.2	154 / 183	9
2012	2.7	139 / 176	8
2013	2.7	136 / 177	8

The EACC also conducts regular anti-corruption surveys. For example, in 2012, the EACC surveyed over 6 400 respondents on, among other things, the incidence, frequency, prevalence, and extent of bribes and unethical conduct in 42 of Kenya's 47 counties.

This survey found that the top six most corrupt public institutions were:

1. The police (48.1%);
2. Traffic police (18.7%);
3. Government hospitals (15.7%);
4. Local authorities (15.4%);
5. The registrar of persons (13.2%); and
6. The provincial administration (10.3%).

The EACC survey also reported that:

- 67% of respondents believed that corruption levels in Kenya were high;
- 60% of respondents had 'observed or witnessed a corrupt act by a public officer' in the previous 12 months, but only 6% reported the incident (Of those who reported the incident, only 11.7% made the report to the EACC);
- 48% believed that the corruption levels were actually increasing;
- 32% believed corruption levels were decreasing;
- 45% did not believe that the Kenyan government was committed to fighting corruption and promoting ethical behaviour in the public service; and
- 35% believed that greed was the leading cause of corruption. (Relatively fewer believed often-mentioned causative factors were responsible, e.g. low pay (12%), culture (11%) and poverty (11%)).

It is worth noting that the level of trust in the EACC and the police is so low that only 6% of corruption incidents are reported to them. This is likely to feed impunity. Also, given that the police are a key institution in access to justice, the rampant corruption in the institution completely compromises the ability of citizens to access justice, despite the relative integrity of the other justice institutions, such as the judiciary.

The Kenyan public widely believes that corruption is one of the primary causes of insecurity. The national assembly often echoes this sentiment with statements to the effect that corruption has grave national security implications and is recognised as a key driver of the collapse of the Kenyan border controls. The joint committee inquiring into the Westgate Mall terror attack of 21 September 2013, which killed 67 and wounded 200, thus concludes in its final report that

> corruption has greatly led to the vulnerability of the country in many cases, including where immigration officials are compromised, thus permitting 'aliens' who could be terrorists to enter the country and acquire identification. This [affords] terrorists ease of movement ... . They are therefore able to plan and execute attacks without fear of discovery. Further compromising of security officials enables [the individuals concerned] to fail to pursue suspected terrorists and enables [such terrorists] to secure early release when caught or reported [as participating] in suspicious criminal activities.[5]

The politics of corruption

Prevention, suppression and punishment of corruption frequently feature in Kenyan political rhetoric, but rarely is this rhetoric matched by action. Kenya has, since independence, consistently seen undertakings being given regarding corruption, only for these undertakings to be followed by inaction.

Analysts note that the levels of campaign financing indicate that the race for political office is partly motivated by profit. A report by Cambridge University found that illegal funds were used to finance the ruling Kenya African National Union's elections in the 1990s.[6] The funds were raised through the Goldenberg affair, whereas those aimed at financing the ruling party's national unity elections in December 2007 were to be raised through the Anglo Leasing scandal. Corrupt campaign financing, therefore, poses a threat to democracy in the country. The democratic space created and expanded by multiparty politics has, however, provided new opportunities for waging the war against corruption. It is in the context of these arguments that the conclusion of this chapter raises broader issues relating to corruption and democracy in Africa.

In the Goldenberg affair, the Kenyan government subsidised fraudulent exports of gold by paying the company, Goldenberg International, 35% more (in Kenyan shillings) than

---

5   Kenya National Assembly (2013) *Report of the Joint Committee on Administration and National Security and Defence and Foreign Relations on the Inquiry into the Westgate Mall Terror Attack, and Other Terrorist Attacks in Mandera in North-Eastern and Kilifi in the Coastal Region.* Available at: http://info.mzalendo.com/ media_root/file_archive/REPORT_OF_THE_COMMITTEE_ON_WESTGATE_ATTACK_-_4.pdf [accessed: 21 September 2014].

6   See: http://journals.cambridge.org/actiondisplayAbstract?fromPage=online&aid=1874776&fileId=S002278X 08003224.

their notional foreign-currency earnings. It is also reported that no gold, or very little gold, was actually exported. It is estimated that the scheme cost Kenya the equivalent of more than 10% of the country's annual gross domestic product (GDP).

The opposition to the Kenya African National Union (KANU)[7] used parliament as a forum to expose the pervasiveness and magnitude of corruption in government. For example, the Goldenberg affair was first exposed by two opposition members of parliament (MPs) who had received whistle-blower information from within the Central Bank of Kenya.

As the opposition consolidated itself, it used the public accounts and public investments committees of parliament (which, according to law, the opposition automatically chaired) to investigate corruption in the government, to devastating effect with regard to the ruling party's credibility. Thus, in October 1999, the Public Accounts Committee (PAC) report was acrimoniously debated in parliament. The speaker of the national assembly at the time, a KANU sinecure, even blocked a public reading of the so-called list of shame, a list which detailed losses suffered ministry by ministry, even though the summary was extracted from the main report.

The report claimed that the government had lost, or not collected, taxes to the staggering amount of over half a trillion Kenyan shillings (USD8.2 billion).[8] It was exposures like these that led directly to the eventual defeat of the KANU in the December 2002 presidential election.

Table 2.2 depicts the extent of the auditor general's queries relating to government expenditure and the conclusions of the PAC.

Kibaki, whose presidency lasted from 2002 to 2013, was initially elected by way of a landslide election victory, in large measure because of his anti-corruption campaign pledges. In his first address to parliament in February 2003, President Kibaki stated:

> Corruption is one of the most serious problems Kenya faces. It has undermined our most important institutions and tarnished our reputations as Kenyan leaders. This is going to change. As president, I intend to lead this change. Corruption, they say, starts at the top. Now the fight against corruption in Kenya will start at the top.

Within a year of his inauguration, 18 allegedly grossly overpriced state security contracts worth a combined USD770 million were concluded with several foreign and domestic entities, which was later to be termed 'Anglo Leasing scandal'. The then permanent secretary in the office of the president, John Githongo, had to go into exile following his exposé of top-level government officials' involvement in the scandal. It was only in March 2015 that 15 accused were charged in court with this flagrant theft of public resources.

A study by the Coalition for Accountable Political Financing (CAPF), a Nairobi-based think tank, estimates that President Mwai Kibaki and Prime Minister Raila Odinga spent USD 75 million on their presidential bids in 2007.

In 2012, *The East African* estimated that the top presidential contenders – such as Uhuru

---

7   The KANU was the political party that formed the government from independence on 12 December 1963 until 27 December 2002.

8   USD8.2 billion is the figure at the prevailing average exchange rate of USD 1=KES 70.

Kenyatta, William Ruto, Raila Odinga, Kalonzo Musyoka, George Saitoti, Peter Kenneth, Raphael Tuju and Martha Karua – could each spend in the range of USD100 million to USD150 million if they were to launch serious national campaigns.

Table 2.2: The PAC Report of 1999[9]

Ministry	Auditor general query (KES)	PAC Report: Amount lost (KES)	PAC Report: Amount lost (USD)[9]
Office of the President	13 479 138 253	4 611 076 104	65 872 516
State House	218 099 055	142 200 484	2 031 435
Directorate of Personnel Management	471 840 595	137 817 650	1 968 824
Foreign Affairs & International Cooperation	2 821 961 313	826 955 373	11 813 658
Home Affairs & National Heritage	262 080 204	103 643 125	1 480 616
Planning & National Development	701 475 795	227 406 635	3 248 666
Defence	928 253 376	278 691 476	3 981 307
Agriculture & Livestock Development	12 743 992 588	4 139 705 624	59 138 652
Health	11 768 641 015	2 334 578 245	33 351 118
Local Government	9 350 069 670	7 914 397 990	113 062 828
Public Works & Housing	5 606 374 768	4 141 970 550	59 171 008
Transport & Communications	15 212 847 638	**	**
**	**	**	**
Total	924 866 342 392	580 475 884 256	8 292 512 632

* Amount of money lost or taxes not collected by these ministries.
** The PAC chairperson, Henry Obwocha, was prevented from reading out the details of any other ministries by the speaker, Francis Ole Kaparo.

During his annual state-of-the-nation address to parliament in 2014, Uhuru Kenyatta, incumbent president of Kenya, stated:

> It remains a hard truth that some of our public services are rife with waste and corruption. That waste threatens the productivity we have so painfully begun to build. I have appointed a cabinet

9   Kenya National Assembly (1999) *Report of the Public Accounts Committee on the Accounts of the Government of Kenya for the Year 1995/1996 Laid on the Table of the House on 8th June 1999.* Kenya National Assembly Official Record (Hansard) 5 October 1999. pp. 1714–1715. Available at: http://books.google.co.za/books?id=kucOiw.
10 The exchange rate in 1999 was USD 1=KES 70.

committee to return us to prudence and probity in public service. The team has already issued a preliminary report, and soon I will give detailed attention to the proposed measures. I also wish to highlight the [overarching] theme that government spending must be brought under control.[11]

D. Civil society, donors and media engagement

The EACC and the public

The EACC has been fairly active in communicating with the public and has sponsored special broadcasts on national and regional radio and television for a number of years. It has partnerships with government departments, semi-autonomous government agencies, and other state corporations in terms of which corruption-reporting boxes are made accessible to the public.

Under the public-education directorate, the commission:

- Conducts county-based outreach clinics;
- Trains public officials within the framework of performance contracting;
- Develops and disseminates information, education and communication materials;
- Mainstreams anti-corruption content in the formal-education system;
- Promotes of integrity clubs in schools; and
- Trains various interest groups in the education and civil-society sectors, among others.

In 2014, the commission carried out public outreach in four counties reaching over 600 000 people directly.

The Media and anti-corruption

Kenya has a well-developed and independent media, by world standards. Since the advent of multiparty politics in the early 1990s, Kenya has consistently reported on corruption and advocated accountability and transparency in the use of public resources.

Indeed, the infamous Goldenberg and Anglo Leasing scandals were made public by courageous reporters despite the best efforts of the respective sitting governments to suppress the affairs by any means necessary.

However, the public's attitude to corrupt leaders seems to place ethnic affiliation above distaste for moral affliction. As a result, corrupt leaders tend to enjoy continued adulation and re-election despite media reports on their illicit activities.

The EACC and donors

In 2014, the EACC reported no partnerships with donors or NGOs. Also worth noting

---

11 State-of-the-nation address to parliament by President Uhuru Kenyatta, 27 March 2014. Available at: http://www.president.go.ke/state-at-the-nation-address-at-parliament-by-h-e-president-uhuru-kenyatta [accessed: 23 July 2014].

is that the EACC received no donor funding despite significant funding gaps. This is an astounding decline from KES126 million (15% of annual expenditure) in 2011.

Civil society and anti-corruption

Kenyan civil society is one of the most robust on the continent. It has consistently agitated for accountability and transparency since the early 1990s. Its activism has, however, not borne the desired results, mainly due to the entrenched nature of corruption in, and impunity of, governments. For example, the KBI has consistently ranked the police as the most corrupt public institution, yet little reform with regard to police accountability has taken place. The incidence of corruption within the institution has consequently not abated over the years.

Donors and anti-corruption

The donor community has been vocal concerning the levels of corruption in Kenya since the early 1990s. In 2014, a former British envoy, Edward Clay, famously complained of the government of Kenya:

> But they can hardly expect us not to care when their gluttony causes them to vomit all over our shoes. Do they really expect us to ignore the lurid and mostly accurate details conveyed in the commendably free media and pursued by a properly-curious parliament?

This was at the onset of the Anglo Leasing scandal mentioned earlier. Unfortunately, his and other donors' concerns were ignored then, and continue to be ignored to this day. This can be attributed to the fact that official donor funding in Kenya constitutes less than 3% of the annual national budget.

E. Commitment to international conventions on corruption

As mentioned above, Kenya ratified the UNCAC on 9 December 2003. On 3 February 2007, it ratified the AU Convention. Kenya is a partner state and has expressed its support of the draft East African Protocol on Preventing and Combating Corruption. The EACC is a founding member of the EAAACA.[12]

Kenya's Constitution provides that 'any treaty or convention ratified by Kenya shall form part of the law of Kenya'.[13] The 2012 Treaty Making and Ratification Act[14] provides for the ratification and repudiation of treaties by Kenya. After the commencement of such Act on 14 December 2012, no person or body can ratify a treaty on behalf of the government of Kenya unless the treaty has been considered and approved by the cabinet and parliament.[15]

The Act requires the cabinet to assess the constitutionality of any proposed treaty and

---

12   For more information about the EAAACA, see its website at http://eaaaca.org/?page_id=16.
13   Constitution of Kenya, 2010, article 2(6).
14   Act No. 45 of 2012.
15   Treaty Making and Ratification Act No. 45 of 2012, section 12.

to consider the financial implications and administrative or legislative requirements before approving it. The Act also establishes a registry and a registrar of treaties whose purpose is to archive and maintain a record: of treaties to which Kenya is a signatory; treaties proposed for ratification by Kenya; treaties that Kenya has ratified; Kenya's reports to any treaty body; and the recommendations and concluding observations of any treaty body on Kenya's reports.[16]

Kenya was the first country to sign and ratify the UNCAC when the convention was opened for ratification in Merida, Mexico, on 9 December 2003.

Domestication of international conventions

As of July 2014, Kenya's national assembly passed the following laws to domesticate the UNCAC and the AU Convention:

- Election Campaign Financing Act, 2013, which was passed and received presidential assent on 24 December 2013;
- Leadership and Integrity Act, 2012;
- Ethics and Anti-Corruption Commission Act, 2011;
- Proceeds of Crime and Anti-Money Laundering Act, 2009;
- Witness Protection Act, 2006;
- Public Officer Ethics Act, 2004; and
- Anti-Corruption and Economic Crimes Act, 2003.

A multisectoral review of progress in implementing chapters 3 and 4 of the UNCAC is under way and the executive is working on a draft Whistle-Blower Protection Bill.[17] Also pending is an Access to Information Bill, which would give effect to such right as conferred by the Constitution.[18] The national assembly is also currently considering a Transfer of Prisoners Bill.[19]

Corruption reporting and international-instrument implementation

A gap analysis of the status of implementation of the UNCAC indicated that, by 2009, there were several areas in which implementation was lacking.

According to the then Minister for Constitutional Affairs and Administration of Justice, Mutula Kilonzo:

> The gap analysis report also shows that there are several measures which Kenya needs to put in place. For example, Kenya has not implemented many of the requirements of chapter 5 of the convention, which provides for measures for asset recovery. There is an urgent need to enact a comprehensive and effective law for the confiscation and forfeiture of proceeds of

---

16 Treaty Making and Ratification Act No. 45 of 2012, section 13 and section 14.
17 Author's interview with Key Informant, TI-Kenya, September 2014.
18 Constitution of Kenya, 2010, article 35.
19 Transfer of Prisoners Bill, 2014, Kenya Gazette Supplement No. 68 (National Assembly Bills No. 23), Nairobi, 16 May 2014. Available at: http://kenyalaw.org/kl/fileadmin/pdfdownloads/bills/2014/ TransferofPrisonersBill2014.pdf [accessed: 23 July 2014].

crime and for the criminalisation of illicit enrichment and money laundering. There is also an urgent need for domestic law on mutual legal assistance, transfer of prisoners and transfer of criminal proceedings. The existing laws on extradition also need to be updated and the usefulness of wealth declarations as an anti-corruption tool should be enhanced by providing for an efficient and effective method of verifying the declarations.

F. Legal framework for preventing and combating corruption

Ethics and Anti-Corruption Commission Act, 2011

This Act establishes the EACC and outlines its functioning, independence and oversight. Though endowed with robust powers of investigation and arrest, the EACC does not have prosecutorial powers.

Election Campaign Financing Act, 2013

This Act was passed and received presidential assent on 24 December 2013. It empowers the EACC to make rules for purposes of administration of the Act and to regulate management, expenditure and accountability in respect of election-campaign funds during election and referendum campaigns, and for related purposes. The Independent Electoral and Boundaries Commission (IEBC) is in the process of developing regulations to implement the Act ahead of the 2017 general elections. The first draft regulations were discussed by stakeholders in April 2014.

The IEBC is initiating the legal reforms early to avoid inconveniences due to late amendments to electoral laws, as was witnessed in the run-up to the 4 March 2013 general elections. Some of the issues that the regulations seek to address include the spending limits for candidates, political parties or referendum committees during the election period. The regulations will also provide guidelines on campaign-financing donations, expenditure, reporting and disclosure, as well as dispute-resolution mechanisms.

Leadership and Integrity Act, 2012

This Act enforces standards of ethics and integrity among public officers. It is intended to give effect to, and establish, procedures and mechanisms for the effective administration of chapter 6 of the Constitution, and for related purposes. The Act obliges state officers to:

- Respect and abide by the Constitution and the law, and lays down that the public trust, and the authority and responsibility, vested in a state officer must be exercised by the state officer in the best interest of the people of Kenya;
- Take personal responsibility for the reasonably foreseeable consequences of any acts or omissions arising from the discharge of the duties of the office;
- Carry out the duties of the office efficiently and honestly, and in a transparent and accountable manner;
- Observe, and subscribe to, ethical and professional requirements;

- Not use the office to unlawfully or wrongfully enrich themselves or any other person;
- Not engage in activities that amount to abuse of office;
- Not misuse public resources;
- Not discriminate against any person;
- Not participate in a tender for the supply of goods or services to a public entity in which they are serving, or with which they are otherwise similarly associated; and
- Not solicit contributions from the public for a public purpose unless the president has, by notice in the gazette, declared a national disaster and allowed a public collection for the purpose of the national disaster in accordance with the law.

Proceeds of Crime and Anti-Money Laundering Act, 2009

Kenya's Anti-Money Laundering and Combating the Financing of Terrorism (AML/CFT) regime had been under review by the International Cooperation Review Group (ICRG) since June 2009. Kenya was initially referred to the ICRG for being a high-risk area/jurisdiction and for its lack of anti-money laundering and terrorist financing laws. Over time, Kenya has addressed the deficiencies that led to the Financial Action Task Force (FATF) review process. Some of the measures that have been introduced include enacting the 2009 Proceeds of Crime and Anti-Money Laundering Act (POCAMLA) and its regulations, which provide for the criminalisation of money laundering and for the establishment of an independent institution responsible for AML/CFT issues, namely the Financial Reporting Centre (FRC). The FRC's objective includes, among other things, assisting in identifying proceeds of crime and combating money laundering.

In 2013, the FRC entered into a memorandum of understanding (MoU) with the respective domestic financial-sector regulators comprising the Central Bank of Kenya, the Capital Markets Authority, the Insurance Regulatory Authority and the Retirement Benefits Authority. The MoU provides for supervision and enforcement of POCAMLA by the supervisors with respect to institutions under their purview. The MoU also provides for the exchange of information that is necessary to support effective anti-money laundering supervision of financial institutions.

Witness Protection Act, 2006

Witness protection remains a fundamental human right under the Bill of Rights (chapter 4) in the Constitution. Also, article 48 guarantees the right to access to justice, while article 50(9) provides for the need to legislate for the protection, rights and welfare of victims of offences. The two articles read together obligate the government to protect witnesses in Kenya.

Section 4 of the Witness Protection Act obligates the witness protection agency concerned to establish and maintain a witness protection programme and further provides for protection measures to be applied by the agency. Sections 13 to 29 of the Act provide for the protection of the identity of the witness. Such protection is secured through:

- Obtaining a new identity for a witness, including recording such identity in the proper registries of birth and marriage (section 13);
- Non-disclosure of a participant's identity (section 22);
- Non-disclosure of the former identity of a protected person (section 23); and
- Non-disclosure of the identity of a participant in legal proceedings (section 24).

Public Officer Ethics Act, 2004

The Act sets forth a code of conduct for public servants. This code is divided into six parts: Part 1 (s 1–4) contains preliminary provisions; part 2 (s 5–6) provides for specific codes of conduct and ethics; part 3 contains a general code of conduct and ethics (s 7–25); part 4 (s 26–34) regulates declarations of income, assets and liabilities; part 5 (s 35–39) deals with enforcement of the code of conduct and ethics; and part 6 (s 40–42) contains general provisions.

Anti-Corruption and Economic Crimes Act, 2003

This specific code calls for selflessness, financial probity, integrity, transparency and accountability.

The general codes in the Act call for instilling public confidence in public office, avoiding conflicts of interest, observing work hours, respecting constitutionalism/the rule of law, and not compromising the public interest.

Access to information

It is indeed challenging to discern and report corruption in an environment of limited access to public information. The right to access public information refers to the right of any person to look for, request, and receive information held by the government.

The Constitution of Kenya provides for access to information under article 35. Thus: (1) Every citizen has the right of access to (a) information held by the state and to (b) information held by another person and required for the exercise or protection of any right or fundamental freedom. (2) Every person has the right to the correction or deletion of untrue or misleading information that affects the person. (3) The state must publish and publicise any important information affecting the nation.

The state is obliged by article 35(3) of the Constitution to publish and publicise any important information affecting the nation; however, the Constitution does not provide any indication of what is deemed to be important information. This absence of such a definition therefore calls for legislation, policies and guidelines in this regard.

Despite the absence of laws governing access to information, the Kenya Open Data Initiative and the Open Governance Partnership make key government data freely available to the public through a single online portal and constitute a country action plan to promote transparency, empower citizens, fight corruption, and harness new technologies to strengthen governance.

G. Ethics and Anti-Corruption Commission

The country's anti-corruption legislation dates back to 1956 and the enactment of the now defunct Prevention of Corruption Act (formerly Cap. 65, LOK). This statute was in operation from August 1956 to May 2003.

Initially, the Prevention of Corruption Act (Cap. 65) was enforced by the police directorate, notably the anti-corruption squad, which was established in 1993. The squad was, however, disbanded in 1995 before it could make any significant impact.

The amendment of the Prevention of Corruption Act (Cap 65, LOK) in early 1997 led to the creation of the Kenya Anti-Corruption Authority (KACA) in 1997.

On 22 December 2000, the high court ruled that the existence of the KACA undermined the powers conferred on both the attorney general and the commissioner of police by the Constitution of the Republic of Kenya.

Subsequently, the Anti-Corruption Police Unit (ACPU) was created by executive order in August 2001, under the criminal investigations department, until the Kenya Anti-Corruption Commission (KACC) was formed in 2003. The KACC was a public body established, on 2 May 2003, under the Anti-Corruption and Economic Crimes Act (ACECA) No. 3 of 2003. The Act also established the Kenya Anti-Corruption Advisory Board, an unincorporated body comprising persons nominated by a cross section of stakeholders. The advisory board made recommendations for appointing a director and assistant directors. It also advised the commission generally on the exercise of its powers and and on the performance of its functions under the Act.

Parliament disbanded the KACC on 24 August 2011, in line with the requirements for change as stipulated in the new constitutional dispensation. The EACC was established after President Kibaki signed the Ethics and Anti-Corruption Commission Act (EACA) on 29 August 2011.

The EACC was established under article 79 of the Constitution of 2010, which provides as follows:

> *Parliament shall enact legislation to establish an independent ethics and anti-corruption commission, which shall be and have the status and powers of a commission under chapter 15, for purposes of ensuring compliance with, and enforcement of, the provisions of chapter 6 of the constitution.*

It is important to note that article 80 of the Constitution also provides that parliament must enact legislation to give effect to the provisions of chapter 6 of the Constitution. Chapter 6 prescribes the constitutional standards of leadership and integrity in public office. It further sets out the responsibilities of leaders, provides for a code of conduct, prescribes the oaths of office, and lays down rules of financial probity in respect of state officers. The national assembly subsequently enacted the EACC in 2011.[20]

Pursuant to the Constitution (2010), the national assembly enacted the EACA to

---

20   The Ethics and Anti-Corruption Commission Act No. 22 of 2011 came into operation (Cap. 65A) commenced on 5 September 2011.

establish the EACC, in place of the former Kenya Anti-Corruption Commission. The EACA codifies the functions and powers of the commission and provides for the qualifications and procedures for the appointment of the chairperson and members of the commission.

Section 11 of the EACA details the functions of the commission as follows:

(1) *In addition to the functions of the commission under article 252 and chapter 6 of the constitution, the commission shall:*

(a) *In relation to state officers;*

(i) *Develop and promote standards and best practices in integrity and anti-corruption;*

(ii) *Develop a code of ethics;*

(b) *Work with other state and public offices in the development and promotion of standards and best practices in integrity and anti-corruption;*

(c) *Receive complaints on the breach of the code of ethics by public officers;*

(d) *Investigate and recommend to the DPP the prosecution of any acts of corruption or violation of codes of ethics or other matter prescribed under this act or any other law enacted pursuant to chapter 6 of the constitution;*

(e) *Recommend appropriate action to be taken against state officers or public officers alleged to have engaged in unethical conduct;*

(f) *Oversee the enforcement of codes of ethics prescribed for public officers;*

(g) *Advise, on its own initiative, any person on any matter within its functions;*

(h) *Raise public awareness on ethical issues and educate the public on the dangers of corruption and enlist and foster public support in combating corruption, but with due regard to the requirements of the Anti-Corruption and Economic Crimes Act (No. 3 of 2003) regarding confidentiality;*

(i) *Subject to article 31 of the constitution, monitor the practices and procedures of public bodies to detect corrupt practices and to secure the revision of methods of work or procedures that may be conducive to corrupt practices; and*

(j) *Institute and conduct proceedings in court for purposes of the recovery or protection of public property, or for the [freezing] or confiscation of proceeds of corruption or related to corruption, or the payment of compensation, or other punitive and disciplinary measures.*

(2) *Any person who contravenes subsection (1)(i) commits an offence.*

(3) *The commission may cooperate and collaborate with other state organs and agencies in the prevention and investigation [of] corruption.*

(4) *The commission shall have all powers necessary or expedient for the efficient and effective execution of its functions under the constitution, this act or any other written law.*

(5) *The commission may request and obtain professional assistance or advice from such persons or organizations as it considers appropriate.*

(6) *The functions of the commissioners shall be to:*

(a) *Assist the commission in policy formulation and ensure that the commission and its* staff, including the secretary, perform their duties to the highest standards possible in accordance with this act;

(b) Give strategic direction to the commission in the performance of its functions as stipulated in this act;

(c) Establish and maintain strategic linkages and partnerships with other stakeholders in the rule of law and other governance sectors;

(d) Deal with reports, complaints of abuse of power, impropriety and other forms of misconduct on the part of the commission or its staff;

(e) Deal with reports of conduct amounting to maladministration, including but not limited to delay in the conduct of investigations and unreasonable invasion of privacy by the commission or its staff.

(7) The commissioners shall meet at least once every quarter, or as often as the need arises for the execution of their functions.

Section 13 of the EACA lists the powers of the Commission as being all powers generally necessary for the execution of its functions under the constitution, the EACA, and any other written law, namely:

1. To educate and create awareness relating to any matter within the commission's mandate;
2. To undertake preventive measures against unethical and corrupt practices;
3. To conduct investigations on its own initiative, or as a result of a complaint made by any person; and
4. To conduct mediation, conciliation and negotiation.

Essentially, the EACC investigates the offences codified in the 2003 Anti-Corruption and Economic Crimes Act. The offences over which the EACC has jurisdiction are as follows:

- Bribery of an agent in either the public or private sectors (s 39 of the ACECA);
- Secret inducements for advice (s 40 of the ACECA);
- Deceiving principals (s 41 of the ACECA);
- Conflicts of interest (s 42 of the ACECA);
- Improper benefits to trustees for appointments (s 43 of the ACECA);
- Bid rigging (s 44 of the ACECA);
- Unlawful handling of public property (s 45 of the ACECA);
- Abuse of office (s 46 of the ACECA); and
- Dealing with suspect property or proceeds of corrupt or criminal conduct (s 47 of the ACECA).

The EACC is operationally independent of both the executive and the legislative branches; however, the EACC is constituted by an appointment process that requires vetting by, and approval of, the national assembly and formal appointment by the president. Removal of a commissioner is also a process involving the president and the national assembly.

Operationally, the EACC must make annual and other periodic reports to the national assembly and the president, as well as be accountable through the auditor general's audit for its use of public funds.

Agency stability

The EACC has consistently been the target of major destabilisation, or threat of destabilisation, since its inception. It is strange that most instances of destabilisation, or threatened destabilisation, seem to coincide with periods when the institution seems to be making progress on politically sensitive cases.

1995: The Anti-Corruption Squad (ACS) is disbanded

The (first) anti-corruption squad constituted in 1993 was disbanded in 1995 before it could make any significant impact.

1998: The director of the KACA, John Harun Mwau, is removed

The amendment of the Prevention of Corruption Act (Cap 65, LOK) in early 1997 led to the creation of the KACA in 1997. The first director was John Harun Mwau, who was appointed in December 1997. After only six months in office, Mwau was suspended and later removed in 1998 through a judicial tribunal appointed by the president at the time, Daniel arap Moi. Justice Aaron G Ringera was appointed to replace him in March 1999.

2000: The KACA is disbanded

On 22 December 2000, the high court in the case of *Gachiengo vs. Republic (2000) 1 EA 52(CAK)* ruled that the existence of the KACA undermined the powers conferred on both the attorney general and the commissioner of police by the Constitution of the Republic of Kenya.

In addition, the high court further held that the statutory provisions establishing the KACA were in conflict with the Constitution. That death knell of the KACA and of various efforts in the fight against corruption in Kenya.

2001: The ACPU is created

The ACPU was created by executive order in August 2001.

2003: The Kenya Anti-Corruption Commission is created

The KACC was a public body established under the ACECA on 2 May 2003. The first director and three assistant directors of the KACC formally took office on 10 September 2004. Wilson Shollei would later fill the vacant position of assistant director of finance and administration.

2009: The KACC directors are removed

Following parliamentary pressure in July 2009, all directors were forced to resign, paving the way for Dr PLO Lumumba to be appointed as director in September 2010. Jane

Onsongo (preventive services) and Pravin Bowry (legal services) joined the existing team of Dr Mutonyi and Wilson Shollei as KACC assistant directors.

2011: The Ethics and Anti-Corruption Commission (EACC) is established

On 24 August 2011, the KACC was disbanded in line with the provisions of the new Constitution. The EACC was established on 29 August 2011.

2012: Several cases are filed against Mumo Matemo

The high court blocked the appointment of Mumo Matemu as chairperson of the EACC on 20 September 2012,[21] but Matemu's appointment was ultimately confirmed on appeal,[22] which reversed the high court decision and concluded his appointment to the EACC.

In questioning the constitutionality of Matemu's appointment, the Trusted Society of Human Rights Alliance argued that Matemu's integrity was impugned by serious allegations of misconduct in his previous career positions with the Agricultural Finance Corporation (a state-owned bank) and with the Kenya Revenue Authority. It pleaded that Matemu's appointment violated article 73 of the Constitution, which requires that state officials be selected 'on the basis of personal integrity, competence, and suitability'. Essentially, the NGO alleged that Matemu was an unfit person to hold office as chairperson of the EACC and ought to be the subject of ongoing criminal investigations.

The NGO further alleged that the national assembly had failed to inquire into credible, unresolved questions about Matemu's past conduct in public-sector employment. It alleged that evidence existed to prove that Matemu's acts and omissions when he held several senior positions at the Agricultural Finance Corporation (AFC), a public body established under the Agricultural Finance Corporation Act (Cap 323), rendered him unsuitable for the position. These allegations included approving loans by the appellant without proper security, involvement in the fraudulent payment of loans to unknown bank accounts, making a false affidavit in a case before the high court, and failure to prevent the loss of public funds entrusted to the AFC.

The second unresolved allegation against Matemu was that, as a senior revenue officer, he failed to collect over KES2.4 billion (USD24 million) due by a tyre-importing company, despite a court judgment in favour of his employer, the Kenya Revenue Authority.

Essentially, it was averred that statutory due process had been followed and that all parties involved in the appointment – in particular the executive and parliament – had noted, discussed, and discounted the allegations brought by the NGO. The petition was opposed by Matemu and other respondents on the following grounds:

---

21 *Trusted Society of Human Rights Alliance vs. Attorney General and Two Others [2012] eKLR.* Available at: http://www.kenyalaw.org/Downloads_FreeCases/88833.pdf [accessed: 21 September 2014]. The decision was handed down on 20 September 2012 by three judges of the high court: Justice Joel Ngugi, Justice Mumbi Ngugi and Justice Odunga.

22 *Mumo Matemu vs. Trusted Society of Human Rights Alliance and Five Others [2013] eKLR.* Available at: http://kenyalaw.org/caselaw/cases/view/84167/ [accessed: 21 September 2014]. The decision was handed down on 26 July 2013 by five judges of the court of appeal: Justice of Appeal, P Kihara Kariuki; Justice of Appeal, W Ouko; Justice of Appeal, PO Kiage; Justice of Appeal, S Gatembu Kairu; and Justice of Appeal, A.K Murgor.

- It was submitted that the NGO lacked locus standi to institute the case;
- It was argued that the petition did not disclose with reasonable certainty the actions complained about and the provisions of the Constitution and the EACA, which were alleged to have been contravened;
- It was urged that the petition be found to be an abuse of the court process, as the NGO had failed to submit its complaints about Matemu's character and integrity to the organs of appointment, that is, to the selection panel, the national assembly and the president; and
- Finally, it was argued that the petition was in contravention of the doctrine of separation of powers, as it constituted an attempt to undertake a *merit review* and not a *procedural review* of the appointment of the appellant.

The Director of Public Prosecutions (DPP) specifically submitted that the petition ought to be dismissed, since Matemu was not under investigation by the DPP, as claimed by the NGO. The DPP further submitted that the DPP had been wrongfully joined in the petition, and that the petition was an afterthought, since the NGO had failed to submit the complaints about Matemu's character and integrity to the organs of appointment.

Appearing as amicus curiae, the Kenya National Commission on Human Rights and the International Commission of Jurists (Kenyan Section) pleaded that 'fulfillment of article 73 of the constitution by members of the EACC was a requirement for the independence of this important constitutional organ'. They submitted that the high court had a duty to use its own objective measure to determine whether parliament had acted in accordance with the Constitution. Such bodies further argued that sufficient documentary evidence had been placed before the high court impugning adherence to constitutional requirements.

The high court found that, as a matter of fact, during the debate on the committee report in the national assembly, there was no attempt to craft a test that would enable the MPs to determine if Matemu had passed the constitutional test under chapter 6 of the Constitution. The court stated that the Constitution obliged the national assembly to investigate the applicant's backgrounds and to 'conclusively consider any information that went to his qualifications' under article 73 of the Constitution.

The court further held that the national assembly had not fulfilled its obligation. It had not followed the prescribed procedure and therefore it was 'not possible to return a verdict that due procedure in an appointment or nomination to a state or public office has been followed when there is absolutely no evidence that the appointing authority considered the constitutional test'. Additionally, 'a procedure cannot be deemed to have been duly followed if it appears from available evidence that the appointment process was designed and executed in such a way that no proper inquiry into pertinent issues related to the qualifications of the appointee was conducted'.

Finally, the court analysed the effect on institutional integrity that Matemu's appointment would have on the EACC. The judges found that Matemu's appointment was made despite allegations he would, as chairperson of the EACC, be expected to investigate. Identifying the obvious conflict of interest, the court concluded that

> it requires no laborious analysis to see that this state of affairs would easily lead many Kenyans to question the impartiality of the commission or impugn its institutional integrity altogether. Were that to happen, it would represent a significant blow to the very institution the interested party is being recruited to head and lead in its institutional growth. In our view, this makes the interested party unsuitable for the position.

On 24 September 2012, Matemu appealed against the decision to the court of appeal in Nairobi, requesting that it issue a declaration (i.e. an order of mandamus) that he was lawfully appointed as the chairperson of the EACC by all the relevant organs of appointment. He further petitioned the court to set aside the entire judgment and all orders made by the high court. In effect, the appeal sought reconfirmation of Matemu's gazetted appointment. The court of appeal conducted an 'intensely fact-based enquiry' and ruled in favour of Matemu, rejecting the conflict-of-interest argument as being based on unproven allegations. The final words of the court in confirming Matemu's suitability to head the official anti-corruption commission were:

> We have examined each of these grounds and our finding is that the evidence before the high court or before us is not probative of any of the claims. We note that the high court itself noted the evidentiary shortcomings by stating that it was not in a position to make any findings whether the above allegations had been proved or not. Therefore, we respectfully hold that the court misdirected itself by concluding that the appellant was unsuitable to hold office, despite its own finding that there had been no conclusive proof of the allegations. It is our considered view that in cases seeking review of an appointment on grounds of the integrity of the appointee, the review cannot be half-hearted. It must be conclusive, fair and just. It was not enough for the high court to state its commitment to an intensely fact-based enquiry, and then proceed to declare that only later legal proceedings would determine the unresolved questions, while still holding the appellant to be unsuitable to hold state office. To do so would be to drown the imperatives of due process, justice and fairness [in] tumultuous waters.

EACC staff

By the end of 2014, the commission had a staff of 264, distributed over five regions of the country.

Recruitment and tenure

The commission appoints, with the approval of the national assembly, a suitably qualified person to be the commission secretary. Section 16(1) of the EACA provides that the recruitment should be transparent and competitive. The commission secretary is the commission's chief executive officer (CEO), as well as its accounting officer. The current holder of this office is responsible for:

- Carrying out the decisions of the commission;
- Day-to-day administration and management of the affairs of the commission;

- Supervision of other employees of the commission; and
- The performance of such duties as may be assigned by the commission.

The commissioners of the EACC are state officers, as per the Constitution, and, as such, cannot be officers of a political party, and cannot run for or hold political or elected offices. The committee of the national assembly that vets nominees should assess the suitability of commissioners based on their qualifications for the office, which are stated in the EACA. The chairperson of the EACC and the two members of the commission are appointed by virtue of the Constitution of Kenya (articles 79 and chapter 6), the EACA, and the Parliamentary Approval Act, No 33 of 2011. The qualifications for appointment to the EACC are set out in section 5 of the EACA.

The chairperson and members of the EACC must also hold a degree from a university recognised in Kenya and must have knowledge of, and experience of not less than 15 years in, any of the following: Ethics and governance, law, public administration, leadership, economics, social studies, auditing, accounting, fraud investigation, public relations and media, and religious studies or philosophy, and must have had a distinguished career in his/her respective field.

The current chairperson, Mumo Matemu, and the two commissioners, Irene Keino and Jane Onsongo, were sworn into office by the chief justice on 5 August 2013 after a long-drawn-out appointment process, which started in September 2011. The process involved lengthy parliamentary debate and, ultimately, litigation, which resulted in a far-reaching decision of the court of appeal on the application of chapter 6 of the Constitution of Kenya to vetting persons nominated to constitutional commissions and other high public offices. The timeline and the process by which the current commissioners were appointed to their offices were as follows:

Following the enactment of the EACA, the president constituted a selection panel that held its inaugural meeting on 12 September 2011. The panel was comprised of representatives of the Office of the President, the Office of the Prime Minister, the Ministry of Justice, National Cohesion and Constitutional Affairs, the Judicial Service Commission, the National Gender and Equality Commission, the Kenya National Commission on Human Rights, the Media Council of Kenya, the Joint Forum of Religious Organisations and the Association of Professional Societies in East Africa.

The selection panel advertised a vacancy for the position of chairperson and two vacancies for the positions of members of the commission in the *Daily Nation* and the *Standard*.

Twenty-one applications were received for the position of chairperson and 164 applications for the positions of members of the commission. However, due to an insufficient number of qualified female applicants for the position of chairperson, the selection panel decided to readvertise the said position.

The names of all the applicants for the positions of members of the commission and the shortlisted candidates were published in the media on 18 October 2011. All interviews for the position of members of the commission were conducted on 1 and 2 November 2011 at the offices of the Public Service Commission.

Readvertising of the position of chairperson was done on 24 October 2011, in the *Daily Nation* and the *Standard*. By the time that applications for the positions closed on 1 November 2011, the selection panel had received a total of 79 applications. Nine candidates for the position of chairperson were shortlisted by the selection panel and their names, as well as the names of all the applicants for the position of chairperson, were published in the print media on 4 November 2011. The public was invited the same day to submit any relevant information on the candidates.

Interviews for the position of chairperson were conducted on 8 and 9 November 2011. The selection panel, pursuant to section 6(5)(e), (f) and (g) of the Act, forwarded to the president three names for the position of chairperson and four names for the positions of members of the commission.

On 24 November 2011, the Office of the Permanent Secretary, Secretary to the Cabinet and Head of Public Service wrote to the clerk of the national assembly indicating that the president had, in consultation with the prime minister, nominated Mumo Matemu as the chairperson, while Dr Jane Kerubo Onsongo and Irene Cheptoo Keino had been nominated as members of the EACC.

On 1 December 2011, the speaker of the national assembly referred the three names to the Departmental Committee on Justice and Legal Affairs for vetting and directed the committee to submit its recommendation to the House by 7 December 2011.

At a meeting held on 14 December 2011, the committee considered the candidates on the basis of the criteria set out in the schedule on public appointment of Parliamentary Approval Act No. 33 of 2011, which lays down criteria for the vetting and approval of nominees for appointment to public office by parliament. The criteria require nominees to disclose information on their personal and professional life, including their political affiliations, tax compliance and potential conflicts of interest, among other things.

On 15 December 2011, the committee reported to the national assembly that, having considered the curricula vitae of all the applicants, it could not support their appointment because they lacked the 'passion, initiative and the drive to lead the fight against corruption in this country'. The report made, however, made no recommendations relating to the unfitness or unsuitability of any of the nominees.

On 20 December 2011, by a division vote of the plenary, the national assembly rejected the committee's report. The deputy speaker used his casting vote in favour of rejecting the report, in effect overturning the recommendation to disapprove the three nominees. The speaker then ruled that the three names could be reintroduced by way of a motion for approval. Five months later, on 10 May 2012, the three nominees were reintroduced before the national assembly and their appointment was approved by acclamation of the plenary. During this debate, allegations of violations of chapter 6 of the Constitution (which deals with leadership and integrity issues) were raised against the proposed chairperson of the commission, but were discounted by the plenary.

The president then appointed the three nominees to their respective positions under

Gazette Notice Number 6602 (Volume CXIV – No. 40), dated 11 May 2012. Four days later, on 15 May 2012, the Trusted Society of Human Rights Alliance filed the petition questioning the constitutionality of the appointment of Mumu Matemu, as detailed above.

Appointment of secretariat staff

The commission's staff are appointed in terms of limited-period contracts that are renewable. This is done through a competitive process and in accordance with the Constitution, applicable laws and a robust internal human resource and administrative system.

Security of tenure

The commissioners of the EACC have security of tenure, and the commission has certain constitutional guarantees. On paper, the Kenyan law grants stability and continuity to the EACC; thus, EACC commissioners serve with security of tenure for six-year terms, which is longer than the terms of the president and the national assembly (five years).

Commissioners can also only be removed by a tribunal following a recommendation by parliament to the president, who then appoints such tribunal.

Capacity

The EACC has its headquarters in Nairobi, Kenya's capital, and has five regional offices in the major towns (Mombasa, Kisumu, Nyeri, Eldoret and Garissa). This is no longer ideal. Since the promulgation of the new Constitution of Kenya in August 2010, the country has devolved public resources and many governmental responsibilities to 47 counties, each of which have an executive (governor) and a legislature (county assembly).

In its 2011/2012 annual report, the commission states that it trained staff in collaboration with the government of Kenya, the United Nations Development Programme (UNDP), the World Bank, and local institutions. An analysis of the scope of training, and of the staff involved in such training, in the 2012/2013 annual report reveals in greater detail who was trained in what field, when the training took place, and whether it was local or foreign-based training.[23] The training programme appears to be ad hoc and generated by requests of staff to attend seminars. Many of these seminars appear to be attended for the purposes of meeting professional accreditation requirements. For example, attendance at Council of Legal Education (CLE) courses is a mandatory requirement for advocates wishing to renew their certificates of practice. Advocates earn points for attending such events. Table 2.3 shows how , in reporting to the national assembly, the EACC includes lawyers attending CLE training, and accountants attending their professional body's annual conferences, in its training. In 2012/2013, the report on training included the attendance of 27 officers as part of continuous legal education. This could have misled MPs as to the actual extent of training actually provided by the EACC.

---

23   EACC (2013) *Ethics and Anti-Corruption Commission Annual Report, 2012–2013*. Nairobi: Ethics and Anti-Corruption Commission. pp. 45–49. Available at: http://www.eacc.go.ke/docs/2012%20-%202013%20 Annual%20Report%20Final.pdf [accessed: 23 July 2014].

Table 2.3: Examples of training from the EACC Report, 2012/2013

Number trained	Subject matter	Venue	Comment
3 Officers	Prevention, analysis and detection of corporate fraud	Eastern and Southern African Management Institute, Arusha, Tanzania 27 May–14 June 2013	Skills in preventing corporate fraud Useful in working with state enterprises and government departments
1 Commissioner	Developing effective policy	London, Englan 24–28 June 2013	
1 Officer	International visitors, leadership programme	Washington DC 22 March–13 April 2013	
3 Officers	Forensic auditing and detecting fraud in the procurement and supply chain	EAAACA Kampala, Uganda 8–19 March 2013	Introduction to forensic auditing and fraud detection in procurement Key for the EACC
1 Officer	Public-sector financial management	Intelligent Africa Marketing and Training, South Africa 26–30 November 2012	
1 Officer	Not stated	OLAF, Brussels, Belgium 19–23 November 2013	Training programme with African partners
1 Officer	Reward management	Eastern and Southern African Management Institute, Durban, South Africa 29 October–9 November 2012	Reward management
1 Officer	UNCAC training in effective legal and practical measures against corruption	JICA, Tokyo, Japan 8 October–14 November 2012	
5 Officers	Trial advocacy in cases of complex crimes	US Department of Justice Office of Overseas Prosecutorial Development and Training 1 & 2 August 2013	
2 Officers	Monitoring and evaluation	AMREF Centre, Nairobi 1–26 July 2013	Does not indicate who conducted the three-week training
8 Officers	Integrated public complaints reporting and referral mechanism (IPCRM)	Nairobi 20–24 May 2013	IPCRM training facilitates complaint referrals for six organisations, apart from the EACC
5 Officers	Investments, realities, opportunities and challenges	Institute of Certified Public Accountants of Kenya (ICPAK), Mombasa, 28 May–1 June 2013	
2 Officers	Continuous professional development seminar: Building professionals in the new dispensation	Kenya Board of Registration of Architects and Quantity Surveyors (BORAQS), Nairobi, 24 May–31 May 2013	

Number trained	Subject matter	Venue	Comment
1 Officer	Professional mediation training	Nairobi, 20–25 May 2013	Does not indicate who conducted the six-day training
2 Officers	Information technology security	Mombasa, 28–30 May 2013	Does not indicate who conducted the three-day training
1 Officer	29th ICPAK annual seminar	Mombasa, 29 May–1 June 2013	
1 Officer	29th ICPAK annual seminar	Continuing Legal Education, Mombasa, 29 & 30 May 2013	CLE
2 Officers	Procurement laws and practices	Continuing Legal Education, Nakuru, 15–18 May 2014	CLE
2 Officers	Legislative-drafting course	Continuing Legal Education, Nairobi, 24 May 2013	CLE
1 Officer	Annual governance and ethics conference	Continuing Legal Education, ICPAK, Mombasa, 9–13 May 2013	CLE
1 Officer	Entry course on arbitration and alternative dispute resolution	Chartered Institute of Arbitrator – Continuous Legal Education, 24 & 25 April 2013	CLE
1 Officer	Supplier and customer relationship management	Institute of Supplies Management, Continuous Legal Education 3–5 April 2013	CLE
2 Officers	Computer forensics, cyber realm investigations, and wireless LAN networks best practices	Continuous Legal Education Mombasa, 25–30 March 2013	CLE
2 Officers	New land laws seminar	Continuous Legal Education, Eldoret, 21 & 22 March 2013	CLE
2 Officers	New land laws seminar	Continuous Legal Education, Nyeri, 21 & 22 February 2013	CLE
1 Officer	Certified information systems auditor training (Kenya College of Accountancy)	Continuous Legal Education, Nairobi, 8 & 9 June 2013	CLE
2 Officers	Practical use of FIDIC conditions of contract: Module one	Continuous Legal Education, Nairobi, 18 & 19 February 2013	CLE
2 Officers	Tactical analysis and dissemination workshop	28–31 January 2013	Does not indicate who conducted the training
1 Officer	Procurement leadership workshop (KISM)	Continuous Legal Education, Mombasa, 5–7 December 2012	CLE

Number trained	Subject matter	Venue	Comment
5 Officers	2nd Interpol Global Programme on Anti-Corruption and Asset Recovery	Interpol, Kenya Institute of Monetary Studies, Nairobi 17–21 December 2012	
2 Officers	Training summit (2012), gala night and awards for excellence	Public Relations Society of Kenya, Continuous Legal Education, Nairobi, 5 & 6 December 2012	Not clear what the training component was
2 Officers	Electoral process laws and practices	Continuous Legal Education, 11 January 2013	CLE
1 Commissioner	Good corporate governance for ethical, effective, productive and sustainable organisations	Mombasa, 21–25 January 2013	Does not state who conducted the training
1 Officer	Seminar on international law: Council for Legal Education (CLE)	Continuous Legal Education, Malindi, 7 December 2012	CLE
1 Officer	Inaugural Forensic Audit Conference	ICPAK, Mombasa, 3–5 October 2012	
1 Officer	2012 Fellows Forum	Institute of Certified Public Secretaries of Kenya (ICPSK), Naivasha, 15–17 November 2012	

Ethics

The chairperson, the two members of the commission and the commission secretary must – within seven days of being sworn into office – sign the Leadership and Integrity Code for State Officers in the EACC. This commits them to abide by the requirements of the Leadership and Integrity Act of 2012. The code covers the following areas and issues:

- Fidelity to the rule of law;
- Respect for public trust;
- Responsibility, performance of duties, and professionalism;
- Financial probity;
- Moral and ethical requirements;
- Treatment of gifts or benefits in kind;
- Conflict of interest;
- Participation in tenders issued by the commission;
- Participation in public collections;
- Prohibition against holding bank accounts outside Kenya;
- Acting on behalf of foreigners;
- Care of official property and misuse of official information;
- Obligation to be politically neutral (through impartiality in the giving of advice);
- Prohibition of other gainful employment;
- Treatment of offers of future employment;

- State officers not to be engaged by the commission until after a two-year cooling-off period;
- Misleading the public and falsification of records;
- Conduct in respect of private affairs, bullying, and dress code;
- Acting through others and reporting improper orders;
- Confidentiality;
- Duty to prevent corruption or unethical practices in carrying out the business of the commission; and
- Promotion of ethics, integrity, and best practices in the fulfilment of the duties of the commission.

The code explicitly states that a breach of its provisions 'amounts to misconduct for which the state officer may be subjected to disciplinary proceedings including, in the case of a violation of chapter 6 or any other provision of the constitution, removal from office' under article 251 of the Constitution. Article 251 provides that a member of a commission may be removed from office only for:
- Serious violation of the Constitution or any other law, including a contravention of chapter 6;
- Gross misconduct, whether in the performance of the member's or office holder's functions, or otherwise;
- Physical or mental incapacity to perform the functions of office;
- Incompetence; or
- Bankruptcy.

In the event of a breach of the code of conduct, which does not amount to a violation of the Constitution, any person may lodge a complaint alleging breach of the code and may submit a petition to the cabinet secretary responsible for the commission (the attorney general). The cabinet secretary must then submit the petition to the president, who, in turn, must constitute an independent review panel to inquire into the allegations contained in the petition in accordance with section 51 of the 2012 Leadership and Integrity Act. The panel is to be comprised of five state officers of good character and integrity drawn from any of the commissions established under chapter 15 of the Constitution. The independent review panel has to inquire into the alleged contravention, and, if the inquiry discloses that a member of the commission has violated chapter 6 of the Constitution, the independent review panel must thereafter take the appropriate disciplinary action, or, if it does not have the power to take the appropriate disciplinary action, refer the matter to a body or person who is vested with the necessary power. Regulations made under section 54(f) will apply to the disciplinary action. A person who is dissatisfied with the decision of the independent review panel may apply for a review within 15 days from the date of the decision. The independent review panel must review its decision within 15 days. A person who is dissatisfied with the decision of the independent review panel may appeal to the high court and the court shall make a decision within 30 days of the appeal.

Section 52 of the 2012 Leadership and Integrity Act provides that the code will apply to all commission staff in pari passu, except that public officers may participate in public collections, conditionally. The third schedule to the EACA also contains another iteration of the codes of conduct, which must – as per section 21 – be signed by all members and employees of the commission.

Section 18 of the EACA establishes the secretariat of the commission and thus the authority and terms of staff recruitment and engagement. It designates the staff of the commission as public officers and makes provision to ensure the diversity of staff. No one gender can therefore be represented in excess of two-thirds of the total staff establishment, and recruitment to the commission must 'reflect [the] ethnic and regional diversity of the people of Kenya'.

Additionally, in accordance with section 34 of the EACA, after the establishment of the EACC, 251 staff of the former KACC, who wanted to be taken on by the new commission. Of these, 236 officers were retained, while the contracts 21 officers were either not renewed or were terminated.

Remuneration

The remuneration of the members of the EACC is generous (see Table 2.4.).

Table 2.4: Approved remuneration structure for staff of the EACC[24]

Grade	Designation	Minimum gross monthly remuneration (KES)	USD	Maximum gross monthly remuneration (KES)	USD
1	Commission Secretary	526 058	6 189	701 441	8 252
2	Deputy Secretary	400 000	4 706	550 000	6 471
3	Chief Officer/Director	300 000	3 529	450 000	5 294
4	Principal Officer/ Deputy Director	230 000	2 706	350 000	4 118
5	Senior Officer/ Assistant Director	180 000	2 118	270 000	3 176
6	Officer I	130 000	1 529	200 000	2 353
7	Officer II	90 000	1 059	130 000	1 529
8	Officer III	80 000	941	120 000	1 412
9	Assistant Officer I	70 000	824	100 000	1 176
10	Assistant Officer II	50 000	588	75 000	882
11	Assistant Officer III	45 000	529	65 000	765
12	Office Assistant	37 000	435	59 000	694

---

24   GA Otieno (2013). Letter to the chairperson of the Ethics and Remuneration Commission. 10 December 2013.

The chairperson's remuneration is KES750 000 (USD8 823) per month; the vice-chairperson earns KES694 000 (USD8 164) per month; and a commissioner earns KES685 000 (USD8 058) per month. The Salaries and Remuneration Commission approved the EACC's remuneration structure for the EACC, as shown in table 2.4.

Despite the Salaries and Remuneration Commission's guidance, some officers who entered into employment prior to December 2013 earn more than the approved remuneration. In particular, including cash allowances and perks, the secretary/CEO's pay is KES930 000 (USD12 400) per month; the deputy secretary of the commission (support services) earns KES655 600 per month (USD7 712); and the deputy secretary (operations) earns KES780 000 per month (USD10 400).

Investigative and prosecutorial powers

The EACC has a clear mandate in terms of the prevention of corruption, as well as the sensitisation and education of the public in the fight against corruption. It also has a statutory mandate to engage with the public in the fight against corruption. Since its establishment, the organisation has invested considerable resources in public-awareness and education campaigns and other efforts, including hosting the International Anti-Corruption Day events celebration in Kenya. It chairs the Kenya Integrity Forum,[25] which convened a national leadership and integrity conference in June 2013, and collaborates with other public-sector institutions, such as educational facilities for outreach to students at junior, tertiary, and higher education levels. The forum also works with professional associations and civil-society organisations in developing codes of conduct and working to improve ethical conduct and introduce better corporate and institutional governance standards.

Despite this, the EACC is not widely relied upon by Kenyans in reporting corruption. For example, a 2012 survey by the commission found that, while 60% of those surveyed had 'observed or witnessed a corrupt act by a public officer' in the past 12 months, only 6% had reported the incident. Of those who reported such incidents, only 11.7% made the report to the EACC.[26]

This is not easily explicable by commission insiders, but it is more likely that the commission is not as ubiquitous a presence as the police and the provincial administration to which the Kenyan public is more used to reporting crimes. The survey thus found that 34% of those who had observed a corrupt act in the 12 preceding months had made a report to the police, and that the provincial administration had received reports from 29% of this segment of the population. Nearly 20% of the respondents did not, in any event, know where to report such incidents, and only 3.6% were able to say that they had 'access to ethics and anti-corruption services in the past one year'.

---

25 EACC (2013) *Conference Resolutions Adopted at the National Leadership and Integrity Conference*. Kenya Integrity Forum, Kenya School of Monetary Studies, Nairobi, 12 June 2013. Available at: http://www.eacc. go.ke/Docs/Resolutions-2013.pdf [accessed: 23 July 2014].

26 EEAC (2014) *National Survey on Corruption and Ethics 2012*. Ethics and Anti-Corruption Commission Research and Planning Department, Directorate of Preventive Services. Available at: http://eacc.go.ke/docs/National-Survey-Corruption-Ethics-2012.pdf [accessed: 23 July 2014].

As stated earlier, the commission does not have prosecutorial powers. Constitutionally, criminal prosecutions may only be conducted by the DPP. However, the DPP may gazette/ designate prosecutors, and has done so in some cases involving the anti-corruption commission, such as in the prosecution of a former minister, Amos Kimunya,[27] and in the extradition proceedings against Samuel Gichuru and Chris Okemo.[28]

The commission, upon concluding that a case warrants prosecution, submits the files to the DPP, who, after assessing the evidence gathered, may initiate a prosecution and file charges, or may return the file requesting further evidence from the commission, or may recommend that the evidence is incapable of sustaining a criminal charge and that the matter should be closed.

The Office of the DPP and the EACC have developed a joint case management system that enables both institutions to keep track of the various files moving between them. In the annual report for 2013, the commission reported that it had forwarded about 1 400 cases to the DPP in that year alone.

In the past, relations between the commission and the DPP were strained and subject to casting blame. However, both the EACC and the DPP have reported that the mutual cooperation between the two institutions was much improved in 2014. Both attribute this improvement in relations to the integrated public complaints referral mechanism which they use for improving and facilitating institutional collaboration.[29]

The EACC's mandate is limited to the public-sector and public funds, but includes state-owned enterprises or private sector entities with public investments in in such enterprises. For example, the EACC mandate would extend to the fiduciary conduct of the national air carrier, Kenya Airways, a publicly traded company in which the government is now a minority shareholder.

The EACC is mandated to engage in civil litigation and negotiations for the purposes of the recovery of assets and proceeds of corrupt conduct. The ACECA of 2003 has provisions that permit asset seizure and the civil recovery of corruptly acquired property.[30] The commission has, through litigation, recovered assets and proceeds of corruption of quite substantial value. Recoveries are banked in a statutory Asset Recovery Fund on which the EACC reports annually to the national assembly and which is audited by the auditor general.

Public-feedback mechanism and witness protection

The EACC has a public-feedback mechanism. After submitting a report, a person has the option of creating an anonymous postbox. From here, that person can access feedback from

---

27   William Korir, 'Kimunya Criminal Case to Continue: High Court', *News24 Kenya*, 8 July 2014. Available
      at: http://m.news24.com/kenya/MyNews24/Kimunya-criminal-case-to-continue-High-Court-20140708
      [accessed: 3 November 2014].
28   See second case study.
29   Author's interview with Key Informants at the EACC and the DPP, June 2014.
30   Anti-Corruption and Economic Crimes Act, 2003 (Cap. 65), part VI, sections 55 and 56. Available at: http://
      www.eacc.go.ke/docs/legal/aceca.pdf [accessed: 23 July 2014].

the EACC on the progress of the report, or receive messages in case there is a need for more clarification and details. This creates a dialogue between the whistle-blower and the EACC, and, since the messages are encrypted, the dialogue remains secure and anonymous.

Financial resources

Together with other ministries and agencies, the EACC bids for annual budgetary allocations in the national budget. The commission does not get allocated what it requests, due to government resource constraints. It is widely recognised, though, that the commission should be better funded. For example, during the debate on the 2014/2015 Appropriation (Budget) Bill, an MP (GW Omondi) stated: 'I would have also liked to see the empowerment of the EACC. This Commission should have been given the money that it requested because we need to know what is going on so that we arrest things that divert us from our development goals.' Nonetheless, the funding of the commission has risen significantly and the institution has grown in terms of human resources and reach in the decade since it was established in 2003.

The controller of budget reports that, for the year 2013, the absorption capacity of the commission was relatively stable year on year. The following table compares first-quarter expenditure of the commission for the financial years 2012 and 2014.

Table 2.5: EACC absorption capacity

EACC analysis of first-quarter recurrent and development expenditure vis-à-vis net exchequer issues (USD)						
Quarter 1 FY 2012–2013	Gross estimates	Net estimates	Exchequer issues	Expenditure	% Exchequer to net estimates	% Expenditure to gross estimates
Recurrent budget	16 000 000	16 000 000	4 000 000	3 000 000	25	18.8
Development budget	2 000 000	2 000 000	0	0	0	2.3

Quarter 1 FY 2013–2014	Gross estimates	Net estimates	Exchequer issues	Expenditure	% Exchequer to net estimates	% Expenditure to gross estimates
Recurrent budget	10 000 000	10 000 000	3 000 000	3 000 000	26.1	25.5

The Kenya National Audit Office annually audits and reports on the accounts of the commission. The audit report comprises an opinion, which may be qualified should there be issues identified in the financial statements that indicate misuse or losses of funds that require further action by the commission or the national assembly.

For example, the 2012/2013 annual report of the EACC contained a qualified opinion by the Kenya National Audit Office, because – bearing in mind materiality – the audit identified

KES5.8 million (USD68 000) worth of irregular personal allowances that were paid to a former chief executive, and that had not been recovered by 30 June 2013, (the last day of the financial year). The audit further revealed that the commission had paid, but could not account for, KES2.9 million (USD34 000) worth of consumable stock (specifically, computer toner cartridges). In addition, the audit found that, as of 30 June 2013 a United Nations-funded wealth declaration management system project had spent KES20.4 million (USD204 000) 'without fully attaining the desired deliverables and goals as spelt out in the project's financing agreement signed on 5 April 2011'.

Table 2.6 details the budget allocation of the EACC for the financial years 2010 to 2013.

Table 2.6: Ethics and Anti-Corruption Commission government of Kenya grants and donor support, 2010–2013

	FY 2013	FY 2012	FY 2011	FY 2010	TOTAL
GOVERNMENT OF KENYA GRANTS					
Recurrent exchequer receipts	12 100 000	12 921 485	13 700 000	14 907 500	53 628 985
Development exchequer receipts	100 000	0	0	0	100 000
DONOR SUPPORT					
UNDP/ADB grants	146 623	131 051	1 264 303	0	1 541 978
GoK grants	0	7 682	650 000	500 000	1 157 682
ADB–GJLOS grants	0	0	0	209 429	209 429
OTHER INCOME					
Sale of tender documents	11 330	4 780	9 130	7 660	32 900
Sale of non-assets and boarded materials documents	320 838	0	0	0	320 838
Interest income	13 539	0	0	0	13 539
TOTAL	12 374 701	13 064 999	15 623 433	15 624 589	56 687 724

Source: EACC (2011) Annual Report, 2010/2011. Nairobi: Ethics and Anti-Corruption Commission. EACC (2012) Annual Report, 2011/2012. Nairobi: Ethics and Anti-Corruption Commission. EACC (2013) Annual Report, 2012/2013. Nairobi: Ethics and Anti-Corruption Commission.

The national assembly's Departmental Committee on the Administration of Justice reviews audit findings and recommendations regarding the EACC, since it deliberates on the commission's budget requests before they are placed before the Budget Committee of the national assembly. The Public Accounts Committee of the national assembly also issues an annual report on the accounts of the EACC based on the audits of the Kenya National Audit Office.

Relationship with the public and other stakeholders

Although, in direct interviews, respondents from the EACC, the DPP's office and civil-society organisations, such as Transparency International, reported good, collaborative working arrangements between the EACC and stakeholders, the real picture is likely to be a little less rosy.

Interviewees confirmed the impression that, among state institutions, there has been a reduction in the turf wars of the past. Former chairperson, Justice Ringera, engaged in public spats with the Office of the Attorney General (and, by extension, the DPP) over the handling of investigations. The DPP maintained that the files passed on by the EACC were not adequate for prosecution purposes, an opinion which provoked the ire of Justice Ringera and the commission on several occasions.[31] In contrast, both the EACC and the DPP tout their much improved working relationship and collaborative report-handling endeavours. It is also fair to say that the relationship between the EACC and some non-state stakeholders[32] is in better shape, and is less antagonistic, than it was under the directorship of Justice Ringera (2003–2008), when relations with the members of civil society became so strained that they actively campaigned against the renewal of his term as director. This is somewhat surprising considering the controversy surrounding the appointment process of the EACC chairperson, Mumo Matemu.

Nonetheless, the latest annual report to parliament by the EACC reveals severe collaboration challenges in the following stark terms:

> The efforts in the fight against corruption by the EACC and other relevant institutions remain uncoordinated and varied due to the absence of national anti-corruption policy to guide the process. This has affected investigation and asset recovery by the EACC, particularly in areas that require an integrated approach among all institutions [that] may be involved in the matter. Thereby, the EACC's capacity to deliver on its mandate is affected. Despite ongoing reforms taking place in the judiciary, the judicial process and adjudication of cases [are] still slow. The EACC continue to be affected by adverse judicial decisions, which stopped investigations or prosecution of cases.[33]

---

31   See, for example: US State Department (2006). Wikileaks. *AG Wako Sends Anglo-Leasing Files Back to KACC: Shell Game Continues.* Nairobi, 27 October 2006. Available at: http://www.wikileaks.org/plusd/cables/06NAIROBI4631_a.html [accessed: 21 September 2014].

32   Notably the Transparency International Kenya Chapter. See, for example, EACC and TI joint courtesy call to the president and the resulting statement by the Office of the President, *Government to work with Transparency International (TI) against corruption,* Nairobi, 19 February 2014. Available at: http://www.president.go.ke/government-to-work-with-transparency-international-ti-against-corruption/ [accessed: 21 September 2014].

33   EACC (2013) *Annual Report 2012/2013.* Nairobi: Ethics and Anti-Corruption Commission. p. xiii. Available at: http://www.eacc.go.ke/docs/2012%20-%202013%20Annual%20Report%20Final.pdf [accessed: 22 September 2014].

During the constitutional review processes ofrom 2008 to 2010, there was a debate between those who wanted an anti-corruption commission with prosecutorial powers and those who wanted criminal prosecution to remain the exclusive mandate of the DPP. In the end, it was the latter view that prevailed. In the final draft of the Constitution, which was put to the vote by way of a referendum, another implicit change was introduced: henceforth, the commissioners would become the executive of the anti-corruption commission and the advisory board would be removed from the structure of the institution. This had far-reaching effects on the accountability of the EACC, which may not have been anticipated at the time.

Relationship with the private sector

The EACC's mandate is restricted to the public sector; thus it has very limited interactions with the private sector.

Kenya's membership of, and participation in, regional anti-corruption bodies

Kenya is a member of the Eastern and Southern African Anti-Money Laundering Group. Moreover, Kenya's law enforcement authorities cooperate through the Eastern Africa Police Chiefs Cooperation Organization. Also, the EACC is a member of the East African Association of Anti-Corruption Authorities (EAAACA).

Reporting mechanism and public perception

The EACC operates a German-designed online whistle-blowing system[34] known as the BKMS.,[35] This system, which is sponsored by way of German bilateral aid through GiZ, facilitates anonymous online corruption reporting. The system is reportedly safe from hacking or other attempts to identify complainants, thus securing whistle-blower protection. The BKMS was designed to escalate corruption complaints within the EACC in order to prevent any officer, or group of officers, from stopping an investigation of reported corruption without reference to the complainant, something which is required by law.[36] While the EACC reports that the system has been a successful intervention, it is difficult to independently verify how the system is actually being used. The obvious difficulty is that an independent auditor would have to have access to the back-end. However, in gaining such access, the auditor be able to identify complainants, or, at the very least, be able to know who the EACC is investigating, which might constitute a breach of the 2003 ACECA.[37]

---

34   KACC (2007) *Annual Report, 2006/2007*, p. 10. Available at: http://eacc.go.ke/Docs/Annual_Report_0607. pdf [accessed: 23 July 2014].

35   Sponsored by the German Development Agency (GiZ), the BKMS (Business Keeper Management System) was implemented by the EACC in 2007. It can be accessed online at http://www.business-keeper.com/ whistleblowing-systems.html.

36   Anti-Corruption and Economic Crimes Act, Cap. 65 Laws of Kenya, 2003, section 25.

37   See Anti-Corruption and Economic Crimes Act, Cap. 65 Laws of Kenya, 2003, section 33.

According to the KBI, 27% of Kenyans encountering bribery did not report such bribery cases, as they believed that no action would be taken. This is an indictment of the justice institutions, including the EACC.

H. The EACC's performance

Investigation and case development

The EACC and its predecessors have investigated and developed cases as illustrated in Table 2.7.

Table 2.7: EACC performance matrix

Year[37]	Complaints received	Investigations arising from complaints	Investigation files forwarded to AG/DPP[38]	Prosecutions approved by the AG/DPP (number)	Prosecutions approved by the AG/DPP (percentage)
2004	3 552	242	0	0	0
2005	3 234	384	35	23	65
2006	7 888	1 150	84	70	83
2007	8 188	1 611	111	70	63
2008[39]	4 485	1 232	86	70	81
2009	4 335	1 270	122	87	71
2010	4 372	1 281	104	75	72
2011	7 106	2 445	134	95	70
2012	5 230	2 183	89	54	60
2013	3 355	1 688	32	28	87

38   Data for the years 2003–2006 taken from Mars Group Kenya, KACC Independent Assessment, Nairobi, 2007, p. 14. Available at: http://publications.marsgroupkenya.org/GAP_Report3_KACC/GAP3_Report_Web_Version.pdf [accessed: 23 July 2014].

39   After promulgation of the Constitution, the responsibility for public prosecutions moved from the Office of the Attorney General to the DPP.

40   Data for 2008–2013 from KACC/EACC annual reports. Available at: http://eacc.go.ke/default.asp?pageid=20 [accessed: 23 July 2014].

Asset recovery

Between 2008 and 2013, the commission reported to parliament that it had recovered property and cash amounting to KES6.8 billion (USD80.4 million). Table 2.8 analyses the amounts recovered in the five years between 2008 and 2013.

Table 2.8: Kenya EACC asset recoveries summary 2010–2013

Year	Value of ongoing asset recovery enquiries during year	Value of assets recovered (KES)	Examples
2012–2013[40]	16.38 billion (USD192.7 million)	567 408 217 (USD6.6 million)	Ministry of Health land valued at KES145 million and Uasin Gishu County Trust land valued at KES80 million
2011–2012[41]	16.285 billion (USD191.58 million)	526 641 044 (USD6.19 million)	Including Mombasa's Uhuru Gardens, a public park
2010–2011[42]	771 710 000 (USD9.078 million)	4 119 218 (USD484 591)	
2009–2010[43]	2.336 billion (USD27.4 million)	1.78 billion (USD20.9 million)	Land reserved for the Kenya Broadcasting Corporation within the Ngong Road Forest Reserve, land forming part of Nairobi National Park, and Kenya Railways Corporation houses in Kisumu
2008–2009[44]	5.61 billion (USD66 million)	144.4 million (USD1.69 million)	Properties recovered were located in Nairobi, Nakuru, Tigoni and Kisii. Most belonged to the Kenya Agricultural Institute and the City Council of Nairobi
2007–2008[45]	[not stated]	3.779 billion (USD44.45 million)	Including recovery of the Grand Regency Hotel, a luxury hotel built with Goldenberg corruption proceeds

41   EACC (2013) Annual Report, 2012/2013. Nairobi: Ethics and Anti-Corruption Commission, p. 15. Available at: http://www.eacc.go.ke/docs/2012%20-%202013%20Annual%20Report%20Final.pdf [accessed: 22 September 2014].

42   EACC (2012) Annual Report, 2011/2012. Nairobi: Ethics and Anti-Corruption Commission. Available at: http://www.eacc.go.ke/docs/EACC%20annual%20report%20-%202011-2012-final.pdf [accessed: 21 September 2014].

43   EACC (2011) Annual Report, 2010/2011. Nairobi: Ethics and Anti-Corruption Commission, p. 21. Available at: http://www.eacc.go.ke/docs/KACC-ANNUAL-REPORT%202010-2011.pdf [accessed: 21 September 2014].

44   KACC (2010) Annual Report, 2009/2010. Nairobi: Kenya Anti-Corruption Commission, p. 29. Available at: http://www.eacc.go.ke/Docs/Annual-Report09-10.pdf [accessed: 21 September 2014].

45   KACC (2009) Annual Report, 2008/2009. Nairobi: Kenya Anti-Corruption Commission, p. 19. Available at: http://www.eacc.go.ke/Docs/KACC-Report-08-09.pdf [accessed: 21 September 2014].

46   KACC (2008) Annual Report, 2007/2008. Nairobi: Kenya Anti-Corruption Commission, p. 12. Available at: http://www.eacc.go.ke/Docs/Annual_Report_0708.pdf [accessed: 21 September 2014].

I. Conclusion

The gulf between words and official action remains. Kenya's leadership over the past decade has been prone to indulge itself in overblown public declarations, such as stating that 'corruption is a crime against humanity,'[47] while condoning corruption when partisan political or economic interests are at play. Kenya's anti-corruption policy is a matter of form exceeding substance. The laws are there, the policy intent and instruments exist, and there is even a rapid and vibrant exposure to 'reaction tango' that has developed between the press and NGOs on the one hand, and the government on the other. The only thing absent is results. For all the activity, Kenya's public service is empirically demonstrated to be corrupt, year after year.

Grand corruption remains a severe challenge to good governance in Kenya. One is tempted to agree in principle with the following statement in the 2012 Anti-Corruption and Ethics Survey Report:

> *Compared [with] international practice, elements of a good anti-corruption strategy exist in Kenya. The country has a solid legislative, regulatory and institutional framework, largely put in place since 2003. The public service utilises good management practices, including a code of conduct, modern employment practices, financial disclosures, fair procurement and a progressive disciplinary system for ensuring economic utilization of all state resources.*

However, Kenya needs to get past the point of celebrating the existence of the legal and institutional instruments needed to fight corruption and start to use these to end its perennial status and ranking as a country in which corruption is rampant. Kenya has never suffered for want of adequate legislation; its problem is impunity and lack of operationalisation of laws and policies.

Kenya's peculiar problem is impunity. This explains why, despite bribery and corruption having been criminalised since 1956, with over a dozen major legislative amendments being enacted to better codify the offences, increase penalties and create new anti-corruption institutions, Kenyans are hard pressed to name a single major corruption prosecution, let alone a conviction, for such notorious crimes. For all the civil-society investment in agitation against corruption, and despite the obviously enlightened Kenyan public seeing the economically deleterious effects of corruption, the menace is not a political issue that wins votes.

Where anti-corruption features as an election issue, it is espoused by every candidate without exception and is cynically appropriated by corrupt politicians who argue that the fact that they have never been convicted by any court means they cannot be held accountable for fairly obvious corrupt or unethical acts. In Kenya, the principle of innocence until guilt has been proven is so grievously abused that the principle's elasticity has been tested to absurd levels, to the point of actually negating chapter 6 of the Constitution.

---

47 Kiraitu Murungi (2003). 'When corruption is a crime against humanity'. Speech delivered at 11th International Anti-Corruption Conference, 25 May 2003. Available at: http://iacconference.org/en/ archive/document/when_corruption_is_a_crime_against_humanity [accessed: 4 November 2015].

The situation is so serious that even the appointment of the chairperson of the EACC is based on a shaky jurisprudence of the court of appeal, which essentially upheld the view that serious allegations are of no consequence in the vetting of public officials and that only convictions by a court count. The court of appeal may have believed that it was raising the standard high enough to protect potential appointees against frivolous and vexatious allegations, which is not an unmeritorious intention, but what it ended up doing was lowering the bar for candidates suitable for public office so patently low that any unconvicted criminal, no matter how notorious their crime, is now eligible for the highest office in the Republic of Kenya.

The court of appeal's decision concerning the Matemu case may very well have followed a prior decision in the matter of Kenyatta and Ruto, in which a challenge against the candidacy of the sitting president and deputy president of Kenya was dismissed, essentially because the court decided to ignore indictments at the International Criminal Court for crimes against humanity when deciding on suitability for nomination to run for president of Kenya. In such an environment, can any anti-corruption institution really be expected to succeed, or is it more likely that it will tread water and seek political signals on how far up it can aim and how wide it can cast its net?

J. Recommendations

In order to address some of these challenges, the following recommendations are being made:

1. Strengthen the overall legal framework for combating corruption

The Independent Advisory Board of the former Anti-Corruption Commission played a useful advisory, control and oversight role that has been lost now that the commissioners are executives and constitute the commission. Ideally, the secretariat should have the benefit of an independent board appointed or nominated, as per the old statute, by stakeholders, with an oversight mandate in respect of the commission and its secretariat (executives). Parliament cannot adequately play this role, as it engages with the commission ex post facto at the end of the year through the audit and budget process, and because it is legally prohibited from having any role in the anti-corruption operations conducted by the EACC. It is obvious why this should be so; no one would want parliament to be involved in the commission's investigative work.

It is therefore recommended that the national assembly should take the necessary legislative action to reinstate, with appropriate modification, an independent oversight body that would represent the public interest in holding the commissioners of the EACC accountable for their work. Rectifying the existing structural weakness will require amendment of the EACA to reinstate the repealed part 3 provisions of the ACECA, and, with appropriate modification, re-establish an independent stakeholder-nominated advisory board[48] to work with the executive commissioners and secretariat in ensuring public confidence and fidelity with regard to the commission's mandate.

It is necessary for the EACC to establish a presence in each county and sub-county if it is to adequately meet the expectations and needs of the majority of the population.

Technology should be to allow greater for public access. The EACC must find ways of enhancing the use of its website, both for corruption reporting and learning. It must invest in web-to-mobile application development so as to take advantage of the growing smartphone penetration in Kenya which constitute (67% of all new mobile devices sold[49]). The commission last reported, that as of 2012, its website had handled 304 unique visitors daily, less than 20% of whom were using Kenyan IP addresses.[50]

2. Strengthen the agency's status (legal framework, appointment, tenure and removal procedures, external oversight, autonomy and independence)

- The EACC should be listed in article 248 of the Constitution so that the question of interpretation does not arise. Getting the EACC listed under article 248 may, however, require a referendum. The supreme court should therefore provide an interpretation of what it would mean to include the EACC under article 248.

- The EACC should be given powers to prosecute. This is in line with Jubilee Manifesto No. 3 and article 157(12) of the Constitution, which allow for delegation of prosecutorial powers by parliament.

- The requirement for the DPP to take on a case once a citizen has begun prosecuting should be removed, with the citizen being allowed to carry the prosecution process forward to the end.

---

48 A review of the nominating bodies is necessary to ensure that the advisory board is as representative as possible. The old advisory board was comprised of 12 members nominated by the following bodies:
1. Law Society of Kenya
2. Institute of Certified Public Accountants of Kenya
3. Kenya Association of Manufacturers
4. Joint Forum of Religious Organisations
5. Federation of Kenya Employers
6. Kenya Bankers Association
7. Central Organisation of Trade Unions
8. Association of Professional Societies in East Africa
9. Architectural Association of Kenya
10. Institution of Engineers of Kenya
11. Kenya Medical Association
12. International Federation of Women Lawyers (Kenya Chapter)

49 C Udemans. '67% of phones sold [are] smartphones.' *Safaricom*, HumanIPO, 21 April 2014. Available at: http://www.humanipo.com/news/42985/kenyas-smartphone-penetration-at-67-safaricom/ [accessed: 3 November 2014].

50 EACC (2102) *Annual Report, 2011–2012.* Nairobi: Ethics and Anti-Corruption Commission, p. 69. Available at: http://www.eacc.go.ke/docs/EACC%20annual%20report%20-%202011-2012-final.pdf [accessed: 3 November 2014].

3. Strengthen the EACC's mandate and interagency collaboration with state and non-state actors and with regional/continental networks

The EACC should focus on asset recovery in order to win public confidence and to justify the resources supplied to it out of the Consolidated Fund. The current EACC is in its first year of operation and is struggling to earn the confidence of a public that is increasingly cynical about the official institutions charged with the fight against corruption in Kenya. Prior to the swearing in of the current commissioners on 5 August 2013, the EACC went without substantive leadership for two years, during which public confidence in the commission all but evaporated. The institution – being leaderless – became moribund and performed poorly. For example, it recovered less than half a million US dollars in two financial years (2010/2011), compared with the previous recovery of USD20.9 million in 2009/2010 and USD6.19 million in the subsequent years (2011/2012).[51] In 2012/2013, it reported recovery ofUSD 6.6 million, mainly comprising land belonging to the government that had been illegally allocated to private entities. The EACC needs to convince the public that there is an anti-corruption dividend in terms of asset recoveries contributing to the public fiscus.

Until Kenya frustrated cooperation in 2009, the Serious Fraud Office (SFO) in the United Kingdom (UK) was investigating UK entities that had received Anglo Leasing scandal-related funds from the government of Kenya. The SFO director at the time indicated that he would consider reopening the investigation if evidence was received from Kenya in the future.[52] Now that the EACC and the attorney general have mutual legal assistance to the Swiss authorities, it is hoped that the same would apply to the UK investigation, which has already obtained evidence from France, Spain and Switzerland.

4. Improve agency financing, independence and sustainability

With regard to financial independence, efforts need to be made to ensure that there is sufficient budgetary and fund allocation to enable the EACC to execute its mandated functions without any delay. Key anti-corruption projects and programmes, like the National Anti-Corruption Strategy and Action Plan (NACSAP), have been reliant on heavy donor funding and, as such, their continuity is not guaranteed. The study therefore recommends that, to the extent possible, the EACC be fully funded from internal resources to avoid the problems caused by the unreliability of donor financing.

---

51 See *Table 2.8: Kenya EACC asset recoveries summary 2010-2013*.
52 Serious Fraud Office (2009) *Anglo Leasing–SFO to Discontinue Probe into Kenyan Contracts*. London: Serious Fraud Office. 4 February 2009. Available at: http://www.sfo.gov.uk/press-room/press-release-archive/press-releases-2009/anglo-leasing---sfo-to-discontinue-probe-into-kenyan-contracts.aspx [accessed: 3 November 2014].

5. Strengthen administration, staff capacity and the infrastructure

- The number of commissioners should be increased to five, with the CEO as an ex officio member. This will reduce the risk of compromise and will also ease decision-making.
- There should also be mechanisms to ensure internal checks and balances, including an internal team that mirrors the work of the commission.
- There should be a schedule to the EACA specifying the relationship between the secretariat and the commissioners. This will reduce risk of conflict by clarifying mandates.

3

Tanzania

A. Executive summary

Tanzania is a signatory and party to global instruments seeking to curb corruption, including the United Nations Convention against Corruption (UNCAC) and the African Union Convention on Preventing and Combating Corruption (AU Convention). These conventions require all signatory member states to put in place mechanisms to address corruption and strengthen the institutions dedicated to preventing and combating corruption. Tanzania is also a member of various anti-corruption organisations.

In 2014, Transparency International's East African Bribery Index ranked Tanzania as the second-most corrupt country within the East African Community. Its experiential survey established that the likelihood of a citizen encountering bribery in the course of a public-service encounter was 19%. A 2005 report by the National Democratic Institute (NDI) noted that electioneering in Tanzania was as expensive as in any other nascent democracy. Political candidates needed to finance 58% of electoral expenses. The NDI report also noted that respondents decried the domination of wealthy individuals who sought office in order to gain access to, and control over, lucrative contracts, and business contributors who demanded paybacks from those whom they supported politically. As a result, the political establishment is often seen as a circle of wealthy individuals who make policy decisions based on private interests, rather than the common good. It thus concluded that a significant proportion of those that wielded political power in Tanzania benefit either directly from corruptly acquired contracts or through contributions from businesses seeking their influence.

Tanzania has a robust anti-corruption legal framework anchored in the Prevention and Combating of Corruption Act and reflected in other laws, like the 2006 Anti-Money Laundering Act (AML), the 2006 Economic and Organised Crimes Control Act, the 2004

Public Procurement Act, and the 2010 Election Expenses Act. The Election Expenses Act prohibits corruption and bribery in elections and requires all candidates and political parties to provide detailed account of their election expenses. The Public Leadership Code of Ethics Act of 1995 (s 9) requires public officials to declare their assets as a mechanism for combating misuse of public resources and corruption in the public service.

In 2007, parliament established the Prevention and Combating of Corruption Bureau (PCCB) by enacting the Prevention and Combating of Corruption Act (PCCA) No. 11. Despite its seeming independence, the PCCB reports directly to the Office of the President. The president also has the power to appoint and remove the director general (DG). Consequently, there is a perception among members of the that patronage by the executive seriously compromises the independence of the PCCB and its ability to perform its functions. The DG has, in the past, expressed frustration with political obstacles placed in the way of the agency's work. Another challenge is the PCCB's reliance on other agencies to detain and prosecute. The DG can authorise an officer of the bureau to conduct an investigation under section 12 of the PCCA. However, the powers to prosecute are still controlled by the director of public prosecutions (DPP), who has the final say as to whether a particular case should be prosecuted or not (s 57 of the PCCA). The DPP also has powers not to prosecute any case by filing a nolle prosequi with the court, as per section 91 of the 1985 Criminal Procedure Act. As a result, out of 5 450 cases, only 473 convictions had been secured by the end of June 2014, representing a mere 8.6% of all the total cases completed. Moreover, a total of 574 cases resulted in acquittals during this period.

In view of the aforegoing, the authors of this chapter commend the government for finally enacting the Whistle Blowers Protection Act (July 2015) as well as the Extractive Industries Transparency and Accountability Act (August 2015). However, the establishment of corruption courts is recommended to ensure expeditious trials in corruption cases. There is also a need to strengthen the PCCB's agency status (e.g. its legal framework, appointment, tenure and removal procedures, external oversight, autonomy and independence)c preferably through the Constitution. We recommend an independent, external oversight structure for the PCCB and moving the PCCB away from the presidency, thus ensuring that it is free of political interference. Finally, we recommend that the PCCB's financing, independence and sustainability be assured through the independence of its budget process, in contrast with the current dependence on the ministerial budget.

B. Introduction

Tanzania is a signatory and party to global instruments and organisations seeking to curb corruption, including the United Nations Convention against Corruption (UNCAC) and the African Union Convention on Preventing and Combating Corruption (AU Convention). These conventions require all signatory member states to put in place mechanisms to address corruption and strengthen the institutions dedicated to preventing and combating corruption. Tanzania is also a member of various anti-corruption organisations.

In 2007, Tanzania passed the Prevention and Combating of Corruption Act (PCCA) and also expanded the powers of the Prevention and Combating of Corruption Bureau (PCCB) as an anti-corruption agency. Nonetheless, there are significant reservations among Tanzanians regarding the effectiveness of the PCCB. It is also worth noting that the PCCB's mandate is limited to mainland Tanzania, leaving Zanzibar to be covered by the Zanzibar Anti-Corruption and Economic Crimes Authority (ZACEA).

The PCCB is often criticised in the media for what is viewed as underperformance in combating corruption. Comments by civil society, politicians and academia suggest that the agency does not enjoy sufficient autonomy to enable it to undertake its mandate. The present study therefore interrogates the validity of these sentiments by examining the state of corruption in Tanzania, as well as PCCB operations. This chapter examines the historical evolution of the legal and institutional framework governing anti-corruption in Tanzania. It assesses the underlying successes and failures of the PCCB in preventing corruption in Tanzania and makes recommendations to strengthen anti-corruption measures in the country.

C. State of corruption

Transparency International's 2014 Corruption Perception Index (CPI) ranked Tanzania 119th out of 175 countries and territories on the global index. The levels of corruption in Tanzania are deemed to be a threat to national security.[53] It is estimated that, between 2001 and 2008, Tanzania lost USD1 billion (TZS1.6 trillion) to corrupt deals. Some of the scandals that have cost the nation tax monies include the following:

- The Bank of Tanzania's 'twin towers' scandal. A 2008 Ernest and Young audit report revealed that more than USD116 million had been improperly paid to 22 firms through the Bank of Tanzania's external payment arrears account in one financial year alone.
- In the Deep Green Finance Ltd scandal, the company was involved in funnelling money between Tangold Ltd and Meremeta Gold Ltd, eventually receiving 'billions of shilling from the Bank of Tanzania within its relatively short lifespan'.[54]
- Tanzania purchased an obsolete radar system costing USD44 million (TZS70 billion) from British Aerospace Engineering (BAE Systems).[55]

The East African Bribery Index of Transparency International in 2014 ranked Tanzania as the second-most corrupt country within the East African Community. Its experiential survey established that the likelihood of a citizen encountering bribery in the course of a public-service encounter was 19% (up from 12.9% in 2013). A disturbing 42% of respondents

---

53   See: http://www.businesstimes.co.tz/index.php?option=com_content&view=article&id=331:poverty-main-threat-to-peace-and-security-in-tanzania&catid=37:column&Itemid=60.
54   See: https://star.worldbank.org/corruption-cases/node/18612.
55   IPP Media (2012) 'Revealed: TZ thieves have Sh315bn in Swiss banks.' *The Guardian*, 23 June 2012. Available at: http://www.ippmedia.com/frontend/index.php?l=42903 [accessed: 28 October 2015].

reported being solicited by public officers for bribes, and an astounding 82% of the public that interacted with the police had bribes demanded of them. Over half of Tanzanians interviewed admitted to having paid a bribe.[56]

A 2009 PCCB survey indicated that 39% of households, 49.7% of company executives and 32.5% of public officials had given bribes to public officers in order to obtain a service.[57]

Despite Transparency International's reports, a PCCB respondent during this enquiry opined that the level of corruption had either been reduced or had generally remained the same. The PCCB notes that the level of grand corruption with impunity has been reduced and that people are generally afraid to engage in grand or massive corruption. It concedes, however, that there is generally widespread corruption in procurement across sectors and especially in the telecommunications sector.

Contrary to the PCCB's opinion that grand corruption is on the wane, incidences of grand corruption continue to emerge. In July 2013, an escrow account for Independent Power Tanzania Ltd (IPTL) showed suspicious transactions amounting to nearly USD122 million, and IPTL is a state company. The controller and auditor general (CAG) found that some of the documents relating to the suspicious transactions were forged and that the withdrawals from IPTL's bank accounts were irregular. Government officials, including ministers, the attorney general and judges are said to have received suspicious payments from one of the former shareholders of IPTL. Parliamentary and public pressure as a result of the report forced the attorney general, Fredrick Werema, to resign, while a cabinet minister, Prof. Anna Tibaijuka, was dismissed by the president. According to the report, Werema and Tibaijuka received TZS1.4 billion and 1.6 billion (approximately USD1 million), respectively, from a former shareholder of IPTL, Mr James Rugemalira.

The politics of corruption

Over the past five years, the fight against corruption has become a politically contestable agenda in most political and policy competitions. In his inaugural speech to parliament in 2005, President Jakaya Kikwete identified fighting corruption as a top priority: 'We will accelerate the war on corruption in a more scientific way, and by addressing its root causes'.[58] While inaugurating the PCCB headquarters in 2009, President Kikwete warned the PCCB officials to either fight corruption or quit.[59]

In 2007, while addressing a public rally at Mwembeyanga in Dar es Salaam, Dr Wilbrod Slaa – then chairperson of the opposition political party Chama Cha Demokrasia na Maendeleo (CHADEMA) – released a so-called list of shame of corruption sharks in Tanzania. The list included high-ranking government and political officials.

56   Transparency International (2014) *Corruption Perceptions Index 2014: Results*. Available at: http://www. transparency.org/cpi2014/results [accessed: 28 October 2015].

57   PCCB (2009) *National Governance and Corruption Survey 2009*. FACEIT in association with Dar Consultants. 21 November 2009.

58   PCCB (2009) *National Governance and Corruption Survey Report 2009* (Vols. 1–4). FACEIT in association with Dar Consultants. 21 November 2009.

59   Agenda Participation 2000 (2009) 'Fight Corruption or Quit, Says JK', *Tanzania Corruption Tracker*, July.

Since the 1995 multiparty elections, the ruling Chama Cha Mapinduzi (CCM) party has campaigned for anti-corruption steps, while at the same time tacitly practising it in its various forms. The Traditional Hospitality Act (2000), popularly known as *takrima*, was defended by the ruling party on the basis that it differs from corruption. In the view of the party leadership, it was meant to ensure that those competing for political posts could extend a vote of thanks to their supporters. The party opined that there is nothing wrong with a parliamentary, or any other elective, candidate providing drinks, food and entertainment for prospective voters as long as these are given in what they describe as good faith.

The financial inequality between ruling-party candidates, on the one hand, and opposition candidates, on the other, has tilted the balance toward incumbent ruling-party candidates. Most of the *takrima* events or activities also involve excessive use of money from unclear or dubious sources. There is thus speculation that candidates are simply agents of businesses for which they have agreed to provide public contracts in in the event of them (the candidates) winning the elections.

On 25 April 2006, the high court of Tanzania declared the Traditional Hospitality Act illegal following a case filed by the Legal and Human Rights Centre (LHRC), Lawyers' Environmental Action Team (LEAT), and the National Organisation for Legal Assistance (NOLA).

The PCCB has since been able to act in respect of electoral malpractices, as outlined in Table 3.1.

Table 3.1: Number of people arrested for corruption relating to CCM preferential polls and elections in 2010

Region	District	Number of people arrested by the PCCB	Cause of arrest
Kilimanjaro	Moshi Urban	4 (including Kasulu District Commissioner Betty Machangu)	Found in possession of TZS150 000 and pairs of *khangas* (i.e. wrapping cloth for women)
Rukwa	Sumbawanga	1	Candidate found in possession of bicycles allegedly distributed to voters in wooing them to vote for him
Arusha	Arusha Urban	21 (including incumbent MP, Felix Mrema)	Found in possession of TZS115 000 and CCM membership cards (some without names and pictures, but already stamped and signed by CCM officials)
Tabora	Tabora East	10 (including Cabinet Minister, Magreth Sitta)	Found in possession of seven mobile phones, TZS1 015 000 and 145 empty envelopes

Source: Various media reports & Agenda Participation 2000 Policy Brief, 2010

A 2005 report by the National Democratic Institute (NDI) noted that electioneering in Tanzania is was expensive as in any other nascent democracy. Political candidates needed to finance 58% of electoral expenses with rallies and events costing 44% of total expenditure. According to the report, most respondents indicated that what made campaigns so expensive in Tanzania was the fact that it had become almost impossible to be elected if a candidate was not willing to spend money either buying votes or influencing her/his party to field her/him in its list. Elections have become more about how much a person is worth and not whether they have policy-relevant ambitions. The report further noted that

> the high cost of elections has turned the political process into something that can only be accessed by rich and predominantly male candidates. This has led to political parties being seen as private businesses rather than vehicles to address certain outstanding policy issues. Parties have formed the habit of nominating only rich candidates who have the capacity to fund their own elections.

The NDI report also noted that respondents decried the domination of wealthy individuals who sought office in order to gain access to, and control over, lucrative contracts, and business contributors who demanded payback from those whom they supported politically. As a result, the political establishment is often seen as a circle of wealthy individuals who make policy decisions based on private interests, rather than the common good.

It thus suffices to conclude that a significant proportion of those who wield political power in Tanzania benefit directly from corruptly acquired contracts or through contributions from businesses seeking their influence.

D. Civil society, donors and media engagement

A few Tanzanian civil-society organisations are currently implementing a series of anti-corruption initiatives. These initiatives include mobilising and training citizens to engage in public expenditure tracking surveys and social accountability monitoring in order to ensure that public resources are utilised appropriately. In 2009, a local civil-society organisation, Agenda Participation 2000, launched the Tanzania corruption-tracking system, which was an online platform for sharing information on corruption in Tanzania.

Tanzania's development partners the United Nations Development Programme (UNDP), United Kingdom, the World Bank, Denmark, Sweden, Switzerland, Finland, Canada, Norway, and the European Union) list combating corruption as an agenda priority. Indicators of the fight against corruption have been included in the processes of Tanzania's General Budget Support (GBS) Performance Assessment Framework (PAF).[60] In 2014, major GBS donors temporarily withheld aid disbursements, requiring that government act on the recommendations of a parliamentary report on alleged corrupt transactions linked to the IPTL-Tegeta escrow account.

---

60 Within the GBS/PAF framework, for example, the government of Tanzania agreed to a results-related indicator requiring it to prepare five cases of grand corruption for prosecution by October 2008. Payments under the new Norwegian and British projects to support tackling grand corruption were to be based upon agreed, results-based performance reports.

Corruption has also dominated in the media. Local newspapers, such as *The Citizen* and *Mawio* (formerly *Mwanahalisi*), have been in the vanguard of reporting cases of corruption through investigative journalism. However, it is considered risky to engage in anti-corruption work in Tanzania. In 2011, Saed Kubenea, the editor of *Mwanahalisi*, was physically assaulted by unknown assailants following editorials and news reports on corruption published his newspaper. The newspaper was later banned by government. In 2012, Absolom Kibanda, editor of the *Mtanzania* newspaper, was also physically attacked and seriously injured by unknown assailants.

The existing, stringent newspaper-registration requirements, as well as official secrets and national security laws, deter media investigation and reporting of sensitive corruption-related cases. A member of parliament, David Kafulia, and *The Citizen* are facing defamation and libel charges in court for blowing the whistle on the alleged fraudulent purchase of assets by IPTL, discussed above.

E. Commitment to international conventions on corruption

Tanzania has signed and ratified a number of relevant international conventions, instruments and protocols relating to corruption. It is a signatory to the UNCAC. This convention was signed by Tanzania on 9 December 2003 and was ratified on 25 May 2005. The government has also ratified the AU Convention and the Southern African Development Community (SADC) Protocol against Corruption. Tanzania has been one of the architects of the East African Community (EAC) anti-corruption protocol, which remains in draft form.[61]

Domestication of international conventions

The UNCAC, the AU Convention, and the SADC Protocol against Corruption have been domesticated through the PCCA. Pursuant to article 11 of the Tanzanian Constitution and articles 9 and 10 of the Tanzanian Law on Treaties (Law No. 24/2000), the AU Convention and the AUCPCC enjoy a special, recognisable status within the laws of the United Republic of Tanzania.

To enhance implementation of these instruments, Tanzania passed the PCCA. In 2012, Zanzibar passed the Zanzibar Anti-Corruption and Economic Crimes Act. This Act establishes the Zanzibar Anti-Corruption and Economic Crimes Authority (ZACEA), with a mandate similar to that of the PCCB on the mainland.

Corruption reporting and the implementation status of international instruments on corruption

Tanzania has submitted a number of reports and has hosted to a number of United Nations (UN) and African Union (AU) verification missions. According to the PCCB's director general, Tanzania is a 'model country' as far as reporting on the implementation of its

---

61   Available at: http://federation.eac.int/index.php?option=com_content&view=article&id=183&Itemid=71..

internationally ratified instruments is concerned. The country has received a number of study missions, including a visit in 2014 by a South African delegation led by Dr Alex Mahapa, deputy director general, Governance and International Relations, South African Ministry of Public Service and Administration. The main purpose of the visit was to learn from South Africa's experience in creating a sustainable anti-corruption agency after the country's apartheid-era anti-corruption agency, the Scorpions, was disbanded. From the available information, it is evident that Tanzania is keen to report on, and demonstrate, the extent to which the internationally ratified instruments have been implemented. The reports are available online for greater public access.

In 2011, Tanzania participated a the pilot review with regard to the UNCAC. The review of Tanzania's implementation of the UNCAC covered nine provisions of the convention and was based on the self-assessment report received from Tanzania, the outcome of dialogue between experts from the Netherlands and the United Kingdom, and an on-site visit between 30 August 2008 and 5 September 2008. The self-assessment analysed Tanzania's anti-corruption systems, legislation and practices relating to the UNCAC's global standards. Among other recommendations, the review mentioned the need for increased capacity building in respect of the agency.[62]

Since 2002, the PCCB has periodically commissioned its own corruption-assessment reports. These reports include the *State of Corruption in Tanzania: Annual Report 2002;* the *National Governance and Corruption Survey 2009* (four volumes); the *National Anti-Corruption Strategy and Action Plan II (NACSAP II) Implementation Report 2009; Taarifa ya Udhibiti na Tafiti Zilizofanyika Mwaka 2008/09* (Research and Control Report 2008/2009); and *Mianya ya Rushwa na uvunaji wa mazao ya misitu, November 2013* (Opportunities for Corruption and Exploitation of Natural Resources, November 2013). All these reports contain key findings and recommendations to improve the implementation of the convention as well as anti-corruption work in Tanzania.

The recommendations contained in the review reports are undermined by the absence of any reference to an independent oversight organ to hold the PCCB accountable. The PCCB has neither an independent oversight board nor independent external organs to which it must account. The agency has linkages with the Good Governance Coordination Unit (GGCU) in the president's office, but it is not clear whether this serves as an oversight body or on a facilitating agency. It is worth noting that direct linkages with the central executive, such as the aforementioned, has often created a negative image of the agency's credibility and independence.

---

62   UNODC. 'Pilot review programme.' Available at: http://www.unodc.org/unodc/en/treaties/CAC/pilot-review. html [accessed: 10 November, 2014] .

F. Legal framework for preventing and combating corruption[63]

Anti-corruption is generally regulated by the PCCA of 2007 and its substantive provisions. The Act provides a broad definition of corruption and of its related offences on section 15 and includes other forms of corruption, like sexual corruption (s 25), as an offence. It punishes both the giver and receiver involved in any form of corruption.

It prohibits corrupt transactions as an inducement to public officials (s 16), corruption in public procurement (s 18), and bribery of foreign officials and organisations (s 18). Possession of unexplained property is an offence under section 27, with embezzlement and misappropriation of public property being an offence under section 28. At face value, the PCCA is a progressive piece of anti-corruption legislation with extensive provisions; however, its effective implementation remains a challenge.

The constitutional regime governing anti-corruption work in Tanzania has been a subject of ongoing debate. The Constitution of Tanzania of 1977 mentions the fight against corruption under article 9(h) of its fundamental objectives and directives of state policy, in which the state commits itself to eradicate all forms of injustice, including corruption. Over the past years, there have, however, been concerns that these provisions are weak and need to be strengthened.

In the last five years, there have been appeals from civil society, citizens, donors and parliament for the PCCB to be given more constitutional autonomy. This was a subject of debate during consideration of the draft constitution by the national assembly in 2013. The initial draft constitution had omitted listing the PCCB as one of the constitutional bodies. After widespread advocacy and public debate, the PCCB was later included as a constitutional body in the draft, which is yet to be ratified by way of a referendum. It is hoped that the PCCB's constitutional status will be maintained in the new constitution. This is also one of the major recommendations of this study.

The anti-corruption regime has been reflected in other laws like the 2006 Anti-Money Laundering Act (AML), the 2006 Economic and Organised Crimes Control Act, the 2004 Public Procurement Act, and the 2010 Election Expenses Act (EEA). The EEA prohibits corruption and bribery in elections and requires all candidates and political parties to provide a detailed account of their election expenses. The Public Leadership Code of Ethics Act of 1995 (s 9) requires public officials to declare their assets as a mechanism for preventing misuse of public resources and corruption in the public service. Effective follow-up and enforcement of this code have remained largely weak. In 2011, the ethics secretariat commissioner, Judge Salome Kaganda, indicated at a press conference that almost half of public servants had

---

63   The legal framework includes the 1958 Prevention of Corruption Ordinance; the 1966 Permanent Commission of Inquiry (Office of the Ombudsman); the 1971 Prevention of Corruption Act; the 1973 Leadership Code; the 1975 amendment to the Prevention of Corruption Act, which provided for the creation of the Prevention of Corruption Bureau (initially, the Prevention of Corruption Squad); the 1983 Campaign against Economic Saboteurs; the 1984 Economic and Organised Crime Control Act; the 1990 Presidential Circular No. 1 on Guidelines for Deterrence of Corruption; the 1995 Law on Ethics for Public Leaders, which established the Commission on Effective Leadership or Ethics Commission (and its amendment of 2001); the 2006 Anti-Money Laundering Act; and the 2007 Prevention and Combating of Corruption Act.

not complied with the law. Political leaders topped the list of non-compliant public officials. Between 2006 and 2009, the ethics secretariat carried out physical verification which revealed that only 1 466 public servants had declared their assets.[64]

The 2001 Public Finance Act (s 25) requires all spending agencies to abide by internationally accepted accounting standards in maintaining records and submitting accounts and reports to the controller and auditor general (CAG) for auditing. The CAG is empowered by law (under the 2008 Public Audit Act) to audit all public expenditures and to ascertain value for money by conducting special and social audits on specific projects. There have been lengthy negotiations to increase transparency in the extractive sector by enacting a new Tanzanian extractive industries transparency initiative (EITI) law. The Extractive Industries Transparency and Accountability Act was finally passed into law in August 2015. Further, there are proposals to amend the 2004 Public Procurement Act (PPA) to enhance its efficacy with regard to corruption. A whistle-blower Bill, intended to protect whistle-blowers and informers, and which had been before parliament since 2011, was finally enacted in August 2015.

The AML Act (s 4) establishes a department known as the Financial Intelligence Unit (FIU) based in the Ministry of Finance. The FIU is responsible (under s 6) for receiving, analysing and disseminating any suspicious-transaction reports and other information regarding potential money laundering or terrorist-financing received. It is supported by a national multidisciplinary committee on anti-money laundering (s 8 of the PCCA) comprising of representatives from various government organs. Despite the symbiosis of the functions of the bodies involved, the PCCB is not a member of this committee, which consequently weakens the bureau's ability to pursue its mandate effectively.

Curbing corruption and public waste features in both Tanzania's Third National Strategy for Reducing Poverty (NGSRP), popularly known as MKUKUTA III, and the five-year National Development Plan. The country's strategy to tackle corruption was articulated in NACSAP II, which ended in 2012. NACSAP III, whose implementation is yet to start, prioritises 'combating corruption in a more scientific way and by addressing its roots causes' as its primary goal.

Access to information

Corruption thrives in an environment of secrecy. It is therefore challenging to detect and measure it with a view to designing and executing appropriate responses. The absence of a law on access to information in Tanzania compromises the ability of law enforcement, oversight and citizen institutions, and individuals to recognise and act on corruption.

G. Prevention and Combating of Corruption Bureau

There are a number of factors which led to the establishment of the bureau. The economic turbulence of the 1960s, 1970s and 1980s made it necessary for the government to contain

---

64   PCCB (2009) *The National Anti-Corruption Strategy and Action Plan-II (NACSAP II) Implementation Report,* Dar es Salaam.

the misuse of public resources. Economic liberalisation and political pressure due to the advent of multiparty politics in the 1990s opened up space for broader debate on corruption and public misuse of the country's resources. Corruption had led to the collapse of major sectors of the economy, including the parastatal sector. Pressure from civil society and the international community to fight corruption led to the formation of the Warioba Commission (named after retired Judge Joseph Warioba) to look into tackling corruption in Tanzania. The commission's report made recommendations for strengthening the legal framework and for establishing a strong anti-corruption body. The combination of these factors played a major role in the establishment of the bureau and its subsequent expansion in 2007.

As discussed above, the PCCB was established by an Act of parliament in 2007 and was mandated by law (i.e. the 2007 Prevention and Combating of Corruption Act No. 11) to prevent corruption, educate society about the effects of corruption, and enforce the law against corruption. The PCCB is an independent public body (s 5 of the PCCA). It replaced the Prevention of Corruption Bureau (PCB), which was established in the 1990s, and the Anti-Corruption (Police) Squad (ACS), established in the 1970s. Despite its seeming independence, the PCCB reports directly to the office of the president. The president also has the power to appoint and remove the PCCB's director general (DG).

In view of its reporting line, public perception exists that patronage by the executive seriously compromises the independence of the PCCB and its ability to perform its task. The DG has, in the past, indicated that lack of political will and political interference are obstacles frustrating the agency's work.[65]

Though its constitutive Act grants permanence and continuity to the bureau, the PCCB is not anchored in the Constitution. This absence of rootedness as a constitutional body makes the PCCB vulnerable to being disbanded without any constitutional amendment process. Moreover, the PCCA is silent on how the bureau may be disbanded.

Historical development of the institutional framework to combat corruption

The legal framework to combat corruption has evolved since the colonial era when Tanganyika (later Tanzania) was governed by the British administration. The Prevention of Corruption Ordinance (PCO) had been used by the British colonial government since the 1930s to punish corruption offenders. This legal regime was repealed by the PCO (Amendment) Act of 1958. In 1970, there was a further development with the passing of the Prevention of Corruption Ordinance (Amendment) Act, and , subsequently, the Prevention of Corruption Act (PCA) , was enacted in 1971.

In 1974, the PCA was amended by Act No 2 of 1974, which established the Anti-Corruption Squad (ACS) by way of Government Notice No. 17 of 1975. The ACS took over the

---

65   These sentiments were expressed by Dr Edward Hosea in his opening remarks at the Pan-African Anti-Corruption Conference: Corruption and Development in Africa, held at the Serena Hotel in Dar es Salaam, Tanzania, on 4 June 2014.

anti-corruption functions which had hitherto been carried out by a specialised branch of the police force. In 1991, following the tide of economic liberalisation and political pluralism, the PCA was further amended through the Prevention of Corruption (Amendment) Act of 1990, which led to the establishment of the Prevention of Corruption Bureau (PCB). In 2007, the PCB was reconstituted as the PCCB.[66]

According to the PCCB, the PCA Cap 329 (RE 2002) had shortcomings that affected the bureau's operations and functioning as a contemporary anti-corruption agency. For example, it was silent about how the agency should execute its functions. Furthermore, it did not provide a legal mandate or opportunity to follow up and prosecute cases, it and did not criminalise most corruption offences, such as trading in influence or possession of unexplained wealth. It was also silent on sexual corruption and other forms of favouritism, which were on the increase.[67] This necessitated a new law and a new institution in 2007.

The ACS and PCB were specialised security and law enforcement agencies designed to promote the economic objectives of the colonial era and of the post-independence *ujamaa* (i.e. socialist) state by tackling corruption and economic crimes. The institutional and legal regime has, however, evolved over time from that of dealing with relatively minor infractions relating to economic objectives during the colonial era to that of combating the sophisticated economic crimes of post-independence governments.

Since its establishment in 2007, the PCCB has not seen significant changes in its powers. Meanwhile, the manifestation and magnitude of corruption has evolved, and continues to rapidly evolve. The PCCB is now required to deal with transnational corruption, sophisticated syndicates, and cybercrime.

Stability of the agency
The PCCB has not experienced any major destabilisation since its inception.

PCCB staff
The PCCB is headed by a DG, assisted by a deputy director general (DDG). The DG and the DDG are both appointed by the president in terms of section 6(2) of the PCCA. The functions of the agency are executed by the DG, DDG, and five directors as heads of directorates. These directorates are the:
- investigations and prosecution (DI);
- research, control and Statistics (DRCS);
- community education (DC);
- planning, monitoring and evaluation (DPME); and
- human resources and administration (DHAR).

The DI is responsible for detecting, investigating and prosecuting corruption offences; the

---

66   PCCB. 'Historical background.' Available at: http://www.pccb.go.tz/index.php/about-pccb/all-about-the-pccb/historical-background [accessed: 29 October 2015].
67   Ibid.

DRCS is responsible for the prevention of corruption in the public and private sectors through the strengthening of systems; the DC is responsible for involving the community in fighting corruption; the DPME is responsible for planning, monitoring and evaluating the activities of the bureau; and the DHAR supports the other directorates by providing them with the right human and other physical and material resources.[68]

The PCCB has no governing council, commission or board; however, some supporters of the current structure argue that it is a law enforcement agency whose functions cannot be subjected to a quasi-political structure, such as a board. They note that some of the cases handled and decisions made are too sensitive to be subjected to a broader organ like a governing council or board.

The absence of a governance board is seen by others as a major internal oversight and accountability deficit, and suggestions are now being proposed for the transformation of the bureau into an anti-corruption commission, which is one of the recommendations of this chapter. The PCCB's organogram is appended as Annex 1 to this report.

Recruitment and tenure

Section 7 of the PCCA mandates the bureau to recruit and employ staff necessary for the efficient performance of the functions of the bureau. The detailed recruitment process in respect of staff at directorate level is not specified in the Act. According to the DG, the heads of the various directorates are recruited openly through a transparent public process. The applicants are subjected to an interview process and screening, and are selected merit. They are further subjected to an internal vetting process before appointment. The PCCB decides their terms and conditions of employment.[69] Critics note that this insular process can be abused and recommend the inclusion of bodies, such as parliament, in the vetting of senior staff.

Security of tenure

The DG's tenure of office is not specified in the PCCA. The DG therefore has no security of tenure and can be removed from his or her office by the president, as the appointing authority. The DG is also required to mandatorily retire at 60 years of age. The staff of the bureau are granted immunity from prosecution for bona fide acts or omissions during the exercise of their functions under the PCCA (s 50).

The PCCA does not provide a detailed process for the removal from office of the head of the bureau or other senior staff. In the event of suspension, dismissal or resignation, the internal PCCB manuals apply. In the event of death or termination of mandate, the president appoints replacements as per section 6(2) of the Act.

The requirements for the recruitment of competent staff are guided by section 7 of the PCCA. However, the process of recruiting staff follows the procedures laid down in the Public

---

68   PCCB. 'Director general welcome message.' Available at: http://www.pccb.go.tz/index.php/about-pccb/all-about-the-pccb/dg-s-welcoming-message [accessed: 30 October 2015].

69   Ibid.

Service Management Act (PSMA). According to the PCCB's reports, the number of staff to be recruited needs to be approved by the public service management office because of its potential impact on the government wage bill, among others. Identified staffing-position needs and public service management office approval are then submitted to the commissioner for budget for the allocation of funds, because the Ministry of Finance has overall responsibility to plan and budget for each financial year. Once approval has been obtained, the recruitment process starts with the advertising of the relevant position, which is followed by shortlisting the top candidates, forming a recruitment committee, interviewing, vetting, and, ultimately, selecting the best candidate and training him or her.

Capacity

The PCCB has over 80 advocates and over 120 legal officers. It also has over 2 086 permanent staff. It has a staff-training plan and has developed an anti-corruption training syllabus that all staff are required to complete. The training programmes comprise a basic course in investigation (three months); an intermediate course in investigation (two months); a senior course in investigation (one month); a command course in investigation (two weeks); and an executive management course (two weeks).

The selection of staff for training and the training programmes are controlled by the bureau. Recruitment of staff for some specialised tasks is classified. Staff are trained both locally and abroad. For example, the Basel Institute on Governance (International Centre for Asset Recovery) has provided training in asset forfeiture.

Remuneration

The remuneration of the bureau's employees is described as 'reasonable' and better than that of mainstream civil servants of the same rank. The salary scales for the PCCB's officers were not available at the time of writing, but the average monthly salaries range between TZS1.5 million to 2.5 million (approximately USD1 000 to USD1 500). The PCCB has, however, expressed concern that the its remuneration of its legal and investigative staff could be lower compared with that of their peers in private practice. The PCCB noted that, if it were given greater constitutional autonomy and political support, further it would be able to access more resources and attract even greater talent.

Ethics

PCCB staff are required to abide by the PCCA and adhere to a code of conduct. Violation of the Act or codes/regulations may lead to action as per the PCCB's internal procedures.

Investigative and prosecutorial powers

The PCCB's mandate is articulated in section 7 of the PCCA. The bureau is tasked with promoting good governance and eradicating corruption. It has powers to examine and advise on matters relating to the prevention of corruption, to solicit public support in the fight against corruption, and to investigate and prosecute offences, on advice from the director of public prosecutions (DPP), as per section 57 of the PCCA. The requirement of clearance by the DPP is seen as a major limitation to the PCCB's performance in dealing with corruption cases in an expeditious manner. It is hoped that the new constitution will broaden the PCCB's mandate to include full prosecutorial powers for all corruption offences.

The PCCB's mandate is limited to mainland Tanzania. Anti-corruption matters in Zanzibar are handled by the ZACEA. The United Republic of Tanzania therefore has two anti-corruption agencies. There is concern that having two agencies dealing with corruption in the same country is a major weakness, as it undermines effective and coordinated efforts against corruption. Multiple anti-corruption agency models have proven a failure in other countries, like Nigeria and South Africa. It is therefore recommended that one agency with a broad mandate covering both the mainland and Zanzibar would be the best option.

The PCCB has a mandate to receive information and reports on corruption. It has toll-free hotlines and secure email addresses for members of the public to report cases of corruption. The location and telephone numbers of all PCCB district and regional offices, and their respective commanders, are widely advertised in the PCCB's media and information material, such as calendars.

The PCCB receives large volumes of information; however, not all information received is sufficient to establish a case of corruption. The decision to act or investigate further depends on the information received. An evaluation is made to determine whether the available information meets the minimum threshold requirements before being subjected to further investigation and action. The minimum threshold is that the information received should show probable and reasonable cause that an offence has been committed.

In support of the PCCB's mandate to investigate all cases of corruption, the DG can authorise an officer of the bureau to conduct a search under section 12 of the PCCA. The powers to prosecute are, however, still vested with the DPP, who makes the final determination as to whether a particular case should be prosecuted or not (s 57 of the PCCA). The DPP also has the power not to proceed with a case by filing a nolle prosequi with the court as per section 91 of the 1985 Criminal Procedure Act.

The aforementioned powers of the DPP have often been a bone of contention between the DPP's office and the PCCB, with the bureau arguing that the DPP's office can sometimes be an obstacle to the speedy prosecution of corruption cases. The PCCB has powers to transfer files from one agency or department to another. According to the PCCB, a total of 1 711 files were transferred to other agencies for further action between 2005 and 2014. Under section 9 of the PCCA, the DG, or any officer, is required to institute criminal proceedings against any person within six months from the date of seizure. In the case of a failure to bring charges against an accused within the six months, an application for extension for another specified period is required. This timeline is also laid down by the Criminal Procedure Act; however, perpetual extension without charge may lead to a miscarriage of justice.

The relationship between the bureau and other law enforcement agencies, like the police, is described as 'good'.[70] The PCCB works with the integrity committees established within the police force to ensure that corruption within the force's ranks is addressed. The bureau also depends on the police to detain those accused of corruption pending arraignment before court and trial. This collaborative relationship is, however, often compromised by the fact that the police have constantly been ranked as the most corrupt institution in Tanzania for the past three years. A PCCB study in 2009 ranked the police force and the judiciary as the most corrupt institutions, with each scoring 64.7% and 58.9%, respectively.[71] Transparency International's 2014 East African Bribery Index also ranked the police force and the judiciary as the most corrupt institutions.

There is a formal relationship between the PCCB and the justice system, including those judicial institutions specialising in dealing with political corruption. There is a legal relationship between the bureau and the DPP, which requires all cases to be forwarded to the DPP for a determination before any prosecution can proceed, as per section 7 of the PCCA and article 59B(2) of the Constitution. The PCCB uses the existing courts to prosecute all corruption cases. A legal relationship also exists between the bureau and the CAG, which requires the CAG to transfer or hand over all suspected cases of corruption to the PCCB for further investigation. The PCCB can also request the CAG to audit any suspected cases of corruption.

There is no formally institutionalised relationship between the PCCB and parliament. As a government agency, the PCCB reports to parliament through the Ministry of Good Governance. Members of the Parliamentary Committee on Constitutional and Legal Affairs regularly visit the bureau to learn and to share information on issues of interest. The last documented visit took place on 29 January 2014. The relationships between the bureau and other parliamentary bodies, like the Tanzanian chapter of the African Parliamentary Network against Corruption (APNAC), are ad hoc and largely built on information sharing and learning. The level of collaboration between parliament and the bureau on corruption matters has been sporadic and, at times, tense. For example, in 2010, the bureau was criticised by parliament for investigating members of parliament suspected of engaging in electoral corruption and fraud.[72]

Public-feedback mechanism and witness protection

The PCCB has no clear feedback mechanism with regard to citizens' complaints. It assures its informers of 'total secrecy' in accordance with section 51 of the PCCA, which prohibits the disclosure of the identity of informers. Also, disclosure of the identity of someone under investigation is an offence under section 37.

The Whistle-Blowers Protection Act was only recently enacted (September 2015). Consequently,

---

70 As per Dr Edward Hosea in an interview with the OSIEA researcher, PCCB headquarters, Dar es Salaam, 19 August 2014.

71 PCCB (2009) *National Governance and Corruption Survey Report 2009* (volumes 1–4). FACEIT in association with Dar Consultants.

72 Agenda Participation 2000 (2010) Are Corruption Tsars plotting to take over parliament?' Article for the Tanzanian Corruption Tracker, Dar es Salaam, 2010.

most witnesses to date have feared disclosure of their identity. Moreover, they are hesitant to appear before courts of law as witnesses, due to a lack of effective witness protection programmes. The PCCB notes that this is one of the factors explaining the low number of citizens coming forward to report corruption or provide tip-offs. It also explains the difficulty in successfully prosecuting current and past corruption cases.

For example, out of 5 450 cases prosecuted since 2008, only 473 convictions had been secured by the end of June 2014, representing a meagre success rate of 8.6%. (For more details on the PCCB's performance and for case statistics, see section H below.)

Witnesses are reluctant to testify in practice and want assurances from the prosecution of personal safety. Some witnesses do not testify or turn hostile. Despite the fact that the PCCB has provisions regarding the protection of witnesses, the bureau still does not have any provisions on the relocation of witnesses, or on the non-disclosure, or limitation of disclosure, of information concerning the identity and whereabouts of such persons. Witness relocation and protection measures are expensive. Therefore the recent passing into law of the the Whistle Blowers Act is to be welcomed. Public officials have a duty to report corruption, but protection up to now has been limited to the provisions of sectio 52 of the PCCA.

Seizure, forfeiture, recovery of assets, and mutual legal assistance

The PCCB has extensive powers to investigate the private sector in terms of section 7 of the PCCA. It also has powers to seize and recover stolen assets section 38 and section 40 of the PCCA. For it to exercise this mandate, the PCCB can collaborate with local and international agencies through the mutual legal assistance procedures provided for in section 39 of the 1991 Mutual Assistance in Criminal Matters Act. The PCCB can also invoke mutual assistance under section 54 of the PCCA, and the extradition of criminals under section 55 of the PCCA. Other related offences are considered under the Extradition Act of 1991. Mutual legal assistance can be afforded for the purposes of identifying, freezing and tracing proceeds of crime in accordance with the provisions of chapter 5 of the UNCAC, which also stipulates that such assistance can be enlisted for the purpose of recovering assets.

In one case, Tanzanian authorities conducted a joint anti-money laundering investigation with India, involving funds stolen from the Central Bank of Tanzania.[73] The Swiss government has also undertaken to support the PCCB in recovering any proven stolen assets held in Swiss banks, but, so far, this cooperation has not materialised.[74]

In recent years, there have been some difficulties in securing mutual legal assistance from certain foreign governments. For instance, the PCCB's request for information from the British Serious Fraud Office (SFO) on the corrupt BAE radar sale to Tanzania, and on assets held in offshore accounts by some public officials, was not honoured.[75] The law is

---

73   UNODC (2011) *UNCAC Tanzania Review 2011*, p. 143.
74   IPP Media (2009) 'Swiss ready to help Tanzania hunt loot.' *The Guardian*, 29 June 2009. Available at: http://www.ippmedia.com/frontend/index.php?l=4035 [accessed: 7 August 2014].
75   JamiiForums (2010) 'Dr Edward Hosea corners SFO.' *The Guardian on Sunday*, 14 February 2010. Available at: http://www.jamiiforums.com/habari-na-hoja-mchanganyiko/52982-dr-edward-hosea-corners-sfo.html [accessed: 30 October 2015].

also silent concerning extradition and mutual assistance in respect of corruption matters involving mainland Tanzania and Zanzibar, given that the PCCA is not applicable in Zanzibar and corruption is not a union matter.

Financial resources

The PCCB's funding is comprised of money appropriated by parliament to cover the bureau's functions (as per s 47 of the PCCA). The bureau is responsible for budgetary planning of its financial resources, based on the ceilings in respect by the Ministry of Finance. The bureau's budget is presented for parliamentary approval through the minister responsible for good governance. The budgetary planning of the bureau is based on the four-year strategic planning cycle, from which an annual plan is extrapolated.

The bureau's access to funds is dependent on releases from the national treasury, and, sometimes, there are delays in disbursement. This affects the bureau's operations. The PCCB has managerial autonomy in respect of its budget and its absorption capacity has been above 90% of the received funds. The bureau's budget is described as 'stable' by the DG, but needs to be increased to ensure greater efficiency.

The PCCB's cash flow is dependent on total revenue collection and disbursements by the central government and donors. No official figures have been provided by the PCCB regarding its total annual budget, but the World Bank estimates that the annual budget for the bureau is around TZS56 billion (around USD27 million).[76] The bureau has received funding from international development partners such as the United Nations Development Programme (UNDP) and the UK Department for Foreign and International Development (DFID). According to the national approved budget allocations, donors contributed over TZS8.1 billion between 2012/2013 and 2014/2015 towards support of key anti-corruption projects under the NACSAP I & II.[77]

Table 3.2: PCCB donor budget allocations and expenditures 2012/2013 through 2014/2015

Item	Description	2012/2013		2013/2014		2014/2015		Donor
		Actual expenditure (TZS)		Approved estimates (TZS)		Approved estimates (TZS)		
Sub-vote	1003 Policy and planning	Local	Forex	Local	Forex	Local	Forex	Grant
6203		-	2 458 900 000	-	1 257 600 000	-	480 000 000	UNDP
6208		-	1 250 000 000	-	1 266 427 000	-	1 455 051 000	DFID

Source: URT (2015) Volume IV: Public Expenditure Estimates Supply Votes (Ministerial) as submitted to the National Assembly 2014/2015: Vote 30: President's Office and Cabinet Secretariat, p. 28.[78]

76   https://www.acauthorities.org/country/tz.
77   URT. (2014) Volume IV: Public Expenditure Estimates Supply Votes (Ministerial) as submitted to the National Assembly 2014/15: Vote 30: President's Office and Cabinet Secretariat, p. 23. Available at: http://www.mof.go.tz/mofdocs/budget/Budget%20Books/2013-2014/Volume%20IV%20Detail%20by%20Vote-Print.pdf.
78   Available at: http://www.mof.go.tz/mofdocs/budget/Budget%20Books/2014_2015/volume%20IV%2ofinal.pdf.

The funds received from government's internal sources are insufficient for the bureau to undertake its mission when one considers the size of the country and the cost of fighting corruption. This has had negative ramifications for the bureau's financial sustainability and for continuity with regard to major anti-corruption projects, which are heavily reliant on donor support. The implementation of NACSAP III has remained stalled because of, among others, lack of approval of funding from the government. The future financial situation of the bureau is uncertain, as the priorities of development partners appear to be shifting from the fight against corruption to other issues, like oil and gas and private-sector support.

Detailed operational budget and auditing

Under section 47(2) of the PCCA, the PCCB is required to keep audited accounts and other records relating to the resources of the bureau. It is required, within three months before the end of each year, to submit financial reports of income and expenditure to the minister responsible for good governance. The reports are supposed to contain a performance report relating to the functions of the bureau. The respective minister is required to present this report to parliament for discussion and approval. The bureau is subjected to an annual audit by the CAG, and, over the past years, it has consistently received an unqualified audit. There are, however, no indications as to whether funds allocated for special operations are subjected to any audit and as to how the reports from these audits are treated. For what are described as 'security reasons', the agency has not been willing to publicly share detailed operational budgets. Requests by the authors for budget frames for the five-year period were declined by the PCCB authorities. There were also no complete operational budget reports documented in the official national budget books. It is therefore difficult to undertake a holistic and independent analysis of the PCCB's financial status in relation to its needs and performance.

Relationship with the public and other stakeholders

The bureau's relationship with the judiciary exists through the integrity committees that have been established within the judiciary. Its relationship with parliament is not formalised, but the bureau has, over time, established a relationship with parliament through visits and through seminar presentations to its committees, like the Constitutional and Legal Affairs Committee and APNAC. Parliament has, in the past, also asked the PCCB to investigate suspected cases of corruption (e.g. in the Richmond case in 2007[79] and the IPTL-Tegeta escrow account case in 2014).

The bureau's relationships with other state organs assume various forms. According to the PCCB, in one corruption case involving the Ministry of Education, the director of

---

79   Richmond Company was contracted to bring in generators to provide 100 megawatts of electricity each day after a drought early in 2006 left low water levels in dams, leading to severe power cuts. But a parliamentary inquiry, launched in November 2007, found that the generators had failed to arrive on time and, when they did arrive, they did not work as required. By the time the company was ready to start operations, Tanzania's power problems had been resolved. Despite these failings, the government paid Richmond more than USD100 000 a day.

personnel cooperated with the PCCB. As a result, the PCCB was able to share information and attend meetings in order to facilitate the investigation and prosecution of the case.[80] In a case involving the Tanzania Revenue Authority, a public servant reported an instance of corruption to the PCCB and the matter was referred to the Public Service Commission.[81] The bureau has also collaborated with the police in making arrests and taking suspects into safe custody. In collaboration with the PCCB, the Integrity Committee of the police force conducts outreach, seminars and workshops with MPs, the press, and religious and community leaders on criminal issues, including corruption.

NACSAP II established the annual National Anti-Corruption Forum (NACF) in November 2008 with the aim of providing a platform for dialogue among all stakeholders on matters of corruption in the public sphere. The forum includes all state integrity institutions, local-government authorities, civil society, the private sector, the media and development partners. The NACF also seeks to inform the general public about stakeholders' achievements and challenges and the way forward. Some of the members of the NACF include representatives from the GGCU, the Leadership Forum, the Office of the Registrar of Political Parties, the Commission of Human Rights and Good Governance, the Legal Sector Reform Programme and the Office of the President – Public Service Management.

The bureau has collaborated with schools to establish anti-corruption clubs in primary and secondary schools. The bureau has also conducted a number of sensitisation seminars on corruption as a way of building greater cooperation between itself and civil society.[82] In 2009, the Policy Forum collaborated with the PCCB in publishing a Swahili booklet *Makosa ya Rushwa katika Uchaguzi* (Corruption Offences in Elections). This was an extract from three different laws, namely the PCCA, the Local Government Elections Act and the National Elections Act. This collaboration, however to be formalised and regularised.

Relationship with the private sector

Under section 46 of the PCCA, the bureau is required to establish and maintain a system of collaboration on corruption issues with the private sector, particularly financial institutions. According to the DG, the bureau encourages the private sector to engage and report any cases of corruption. So far, the private sector has not fully taken up this offer. In 2008, the PCCB's collaboration with the private sector established Business Action Against Corruption (BAAC). However, this body is not very active and its results are yet to be seen.

A system for blacklisting companies convicted of corruption exists. Once a company is found to have been involved in corruption and to be in contravention of the Public Procurement Act No. 21 of 2004, section 57, the company will be blacklisted and barred from further tenders. Examples of companies blacklisted in terms of this framework

---

80   URT (2015) Volume IV: Public Expenditure Estimates Supply Votes (Ministerial) as submitted to the National Assembly 2014/15: Vote 30: President's Office and Cabinet Secretariat, p. 28.
81   Ibid.
82   PCCB (2012) *The National Anti-Corruption Strategy and Action Plan-II (NACSAP II) Implementation Report*, Dar es Salaam.

include Oxford University Press East Africa Ltd; Oxford University Press Tanzania Ldt; China Communications Construction Company Ltd; and China Geo-Engineering Corporation.[83] These companies were involved in corruption in order to secure government tenders. However, there is inadequate interagency collaboration to ensure that blacklisted companies do not win government procurement tenders elsewhere. For example, the above-mentioned companies are all still operational in the country and some have since won more government tenders. One of the blacklisted Chinese companies won a tender to construct the port of Dar es Salaam.

Financial institutions are required to cooperate with the PCCB on matters related to corruption in terms of section 48 of the Banking and Financial Institutions Act.

Donors provide the bureau with technical and financial. Donors funded the NASCAP I & II programmes, with over TZS8 billion being disbursed on anti-corruption measures between 2012/2013 and 2014/2015. The PCCB was the lead organisation in the implementation of these programmes. The PCCB reports on the progress of these programmes during the annual GBS review meetings. On 31 December 2013, the PCCB received a donation of property and equipment worth TZS400 million from the Chinese government. In addition, the DFID has supported training in criminal justice and has built the capacity of the PCCB's staff with regard to financial investigations and asset recovery.

Tanzania's membership of, and participation in, regional anti-corruption bodies
Tanzania is a member of the Eastern and Southern African Anti-Money Laundering Group, and, through this, the PCCB has been peer-reviewed. Among other suggestions, the review recommends further capacity building in the areas of investigation and prosecution. The most recent mutual evaluation can be found at http://www.esaamlg.org/reports/me.php. Tanzanian law enforcement authorities cooperate through the Southern African Regional Police Chiefs Cooperation Organisation and through the Eastern Africa Police Chiefs Cooperation Organisation. The PCCB is also a member of the Southern Africa Forum Against Corruption (SAFAC) and the PCCB's DG was SAFAC's chair between 2010 and 2011. The PCCB is a member of the East African Association of Anti-Corruption Authorities and Tanzania is the current president of the association. The PCCB's DG has also served on the AU's anti-corruption advisory board.

Reporting mechanism and public perception
From a legal standpoint, the PCCB falls within the ambit of the president's office and thus the bureau is required by law (s 14 of the PCCA) to submit its report to the president on or before 31 March of every year, or at such later date as the president may determine. The minister responsible for good governance also receives the PCCB reports, as per section 48 of the PCCA. The minister responsible is required to present these reports to parliament for discussion. The quality of discussion on these reports is often compromised

---

83   UNODC (2011) *UNCAC Tanzania Review 2011.*

because of limited knowledge of corruption matters and inadequate advance preparation and insufficient information provided for parliamentarians. Also, the time allocated for discussion of these reports is often limited due to the congested parliamentary schedule.

The bureau does not have a clear mechanism for objectively assessing public perceptions of its performance. According to the DG, these are just perceptions without objective truth and are quite often based on misinformation or lack of extensive knowledge of the sector. The bureau listens and sometimes acts on these perceptions, but it is not entirely driven by what the public says. The agency has commissioned a study to establish its own indicators for measuring the level of corruption in the country. This report is expected to be released before the end of 2015.

The bureau has a well-established physical infrastructure, including fully furnished headquarters in Dar es Salaam. The PCCB has sub-offices located in 24 regions and in all districts of mainland Tanzania. The PCCB has widely publicised their locations and the contact numbers of the respective district commanders as a strategy for increasing public access and the reporting of corruption.

The bureau has had a long-term working relationship with donors. Since 2012, the UNDP has contributed over TZS4.2 billion to the PCCB. The DFID has provided a further TZS3.9 billion towards strengthening anti-corruption work in the country.[84] The international community has also provided training and technical expertise. However, the relationship with donors has at times been strained, particularly when they request the PCCB to deliver better results. In 2011, the development partners withheld aid, demanding that the government prosecute grand-corruption cases. Speaking at the GBS annual review meeting, Svein Baera, Minister Counsellor of the Royal Norwegian Embassy and chair of the Development Partners Group, stated that the fight against petty and grand corruption was 'unsatisfactory' and sought evidence of the progress made. Development partners chose not to commit themselves on disbursing aid for general budget support. As mentioned above, in 2014, the development partners temporarily withheld aid due to corruption allegations surrounding the IPTL-Tegeta escrow account.

H. The PCCB's performance

The key strength of the bureau lies in its expansion over the past years. The organisation now has a presence in most parts of mainland Tanzania. During this period, the head of government has been supportive of the bureau, constantly urging it to deliver results. At the time of writing, the PCCB had over 2 086 permanent staff. However, the major challenge has been how to translate this infrastructure into effective machinery to combat corruption.

Case management and resources recovered

The number of successful prosecutions and rhe value of resources recovered by the bureau

---

84 UNODC (2011) *UNCAC Tanzania Review 2011.*

over the past six years are still low. According to the PCCB's case statistics, 473 convictions were secured and TZS86.6 billion recovered for the period between 2005 and June 2014.[85] Approximately TZS93 billion, roughly equivalent to USD59 million, has been recovered since 1995.

In 2011, the PCCB recovered TZS4.639 billion (USD3 million); in 2010, TZS10.123 billion (USD6.7 million); in 2009, TZS436 million (USD290 000); and TZS13.204 billion (USD8.8 million) in 2008.[86] Of the total recovered, it is not clear how much was from grand-corruption cases like the Bank of Tanzania–External Payment Accounts (BOT-EPA) scandal in 2005. It is also not clear how much has been recovered from corrupt dealings and savings in offshore accounts or assets frozen from outside Tanzania.

Table 3.3: Case atistics and resources recovered, 2005–June 2014 (*USD equivalent)

YEARS	*Allegations Received	Cases investigated	Completed investigation files	Administrative actions taken	Files transferred to other agencies	Files sent to DPP	New cases into courts	Total cases prosecuted	Conviction cases	Acquittal cases	Money saved/assets recovered
2005	3 121	677	540	111	2	20	50	218	6	10	2 500 600 000
2006	6 320	1 528	1 781	209	496	22	71	251	18	28	1 301 49 528
2007	8 235	1 266	1 966	280	460	38	196	352	35	45	1 580 099 081
2008	6 137	928	1 038	74	184	119	147	416	37	71	13 203 459 357
2009	5 930	884	1 188	40	152	156	222	463	46	73	436 132 336
2010	5 685	870	924	29	135	112	224	587	56	98	10 123 258 300
2011	4 765	819	868	30	84	143	193	709	52	61	4 638 939 558
2012	5 084	1 178	881	27	72	221	288	723	47	71	9 667 354 594
2013	5 456	1 100	1 027	19	98	358	343	894	89	62	4 235 401 591
(January –June) 2014	2 765	391	415	6	28	143	166	837	87	55	38 959 726 644
TOTAL	53 498	9 641	10 628	825	1 711	1 368	1 900	5 450*	473*	574	86 671 105 989

Source: PCCB – interview with key informant, Head Office, September, 2014.
* These figures have been corrected from the original figures from the PCCB, which had some errors in the calculations.

---

85   PCCB statistics available at: http://www.pccb.go.tz/index.php/investigation/sport-news/case-statistics/579-statistics-as-from-2005-to-june-2014 [accessed: 2 November 2015].
86   UNODC (2011) *UNCAC Tanzania Review 2011*, p. 34.

The PCCB data indicates that, by the end of 2008, the number of cases filed in court increased to 1 900 from a mere 147 cases handled under the old PCA. Despite the increase in the amount of money recovered and in the number of cases filed in courts, the PCCB still faces a daunting challenge of low conviction rates. According to the data, out of 5 450 cases, only 473 convictions had been secured by the end of June 2014, representing a mere 8.6% of the total prosecutions completed. A total of 574 cases were acquittals, representing 10.5% of the total prosecutions for the period.

The number of administrative actions taken against public servants for corrupt behaviour from 2005 to December 2014 was 825. This represents 7.8% of all completed investigations carried out by the PCCB for the period. The highest number of cases of administrative action was that between 2005 and 2007. However, this data does not indicate the cadre of public servants who are more prone to or inclined towards corruption. There is no information regarding the nature of the administrative action taken. Quite often, the administrative action taken involved written warnings or the transfer of errant public servants from one department to another, or from one geographical area to another. The consequence of these actions is that corruption may be spread across departments and geographical locations.

Figure 3.1: Comparison of prosecutions, convictions and acquittals in PCCB corruption cases, 2005–2014.

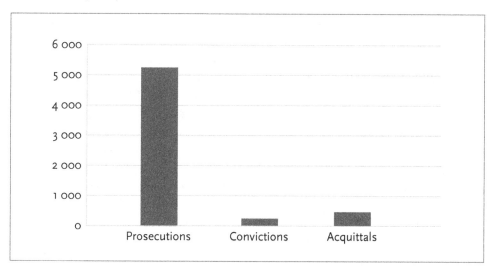

Over the past few years, the PCCB has faced criticism from civil society and parliament for non-performance and arguments that the assets recovered and the convictions secured do not adequately reflect the magnitude of corruption in the country. The volume of funds recovered so far is low compared with what is estimated to have been lost. For example, the TZS93 billion (USD 62 million) recovered between 1995 and 2014 compares poorly with the approximately TZS193 billion (USD128 million) lost in the combined BOT–EPA scandal and infamous military radar purchase alone.

There have been concerns regarding the general slackening in the prosecution of cases and the lack of funding to prosecute some corruption cases. In 2012, chief justice Othman Chande threatened to send back election-corruption cases to parliament for lack of funds to prosecute them. Since the chief justice's treat, it is not evident what remedial measure has been taken by government to boost the judiciary's financial capacity to prosecute these cases. On average, it takes 680 days (over two years) to investigate and prosecute a single election case.

Table 3.4: Cases of election corruption on mainland Tanzania reported and investigated before, during and after the 2010 general elections

1	Electoral incidences reported	41
2	Number of cases filed in court	23
3	Number of cases concluded to date	18
4	Number of cases withdrawn	01
5	Number of cases pending in courts of law	04
6	Type of court verdicts for concluded cases: Convictions Acquittals	 7 11
7	Average number of days taken per case	680

Source: PCCB Headquarters, September 2014

According to the PCCB, some of its problems can be traced back to the office of the DPP and to the judiciary, whose mandates involve prosecuting and hearing cases referred to them by the bureau. They are, it is argued, not acting fast enough to prosecute and decide corruption cases. Once cases are with the DPP and the judiciary, the PCCB has very little say. The PCCB mandate ends here.[87]

Despite its challenges, the PCCB has had successful investigations and prosecutions. One such cases was the matter of Amatus Liyumba,[88] a former director of personnel and administration at the Bank of Tanzania. Liyumba was successfully prosecuted and convicted for corruption and abuse of power, and for causing financial loss to the government. The court found that Liyumba had arbitrarily taken major decisions in altering the scope of work on a construction project financed by the Bank of Tanzania. As a result of these unilateral changes, the cost of the construction project rose from about USD73 million to USD357 675 568. The accused was sentenced to serve two years in jail. Other cases which the state won include: *Republic vs. John Kinyaki Nembo*, Criminal Case No. 09/2010; *Republic vs. Mohamed Ali*,

---

87   Based on the opening remarks of Dr Edward Hosea at the Pan-African Anti-Corruption Conference: Corruption and Development in Africa, held at the Serena Hotel in Dar es Salaam, Tanzania, 4 June 2013.

88   See *Republic vs. Amatus Liyumba*, Criminal Case No.105/2009.

Criminal Case No. 302/2010; *Republic vs. Jamila Nzota*, Criminal Case No. 1090/2009; and *Republic vs. Jaqueline Basilo Shazi*, Criminal Case No. 280/2009. The most recent case was the successful prosecution and conviction in August 2014 of the former Tanzania Bureau of Standards (TBS) DG, Charles Ekerege, who was sentenced to a three-year jail term for abuse of office leading to a loss to the government of over TZS70.2million through a bogus motor vehicle inspection programme abroad.

The PCCB has also experienced incidences of poor prosecution and political interference. An example is the case of the *Republic vs. Costa Mahalu and others* (Economic Criminal Case No. 1 of 2007. Costa Ricky Mahalu, a former ambassador to Italy, and his assistant, Grace Alfred Martin, were prosecuted for making suspicious payments relating to the purchase of Tanzania's chancery in Italy. It was alleged that the two conspired and ultimately misled their principal, resulting in a loss to the government. This was in violation of the PCCA (Cap. 16 R.E. 2002) and the Economic and Organised Crimes Control Act (Cap 2000 RE. 2002).[89]

The purchase was done through two contracts executed on the same day, but for different prices. The first contract was executed before a notary public of Italy, Marco Papi, which showed that the purchase price was EUR1 032 913.80. The second contract executed between the vendor and the ambassador, but which was not witnessed by a notary public, showed that the purchase price was EUR3 098 741.40. According to bank statements tendered as exhibits in court, the payment of the purchase price was made on 24 September 2002 into two separate accounts, both of CERES S.R.L. The exhibits showed that a payment for EUR2 065 827.60 was made, and that another payment for EUR1 032 913.80 was deposited into a second account, in Rome. Upon signing the contracts and having confirmed receipt of the money on 1 October 2002, the vendor issued a payment receipt for EUR3 098 741.40. On 23 September 2002, the embassy had issued a payment voucher authorising payment of EUR3 098 741.40 to CERES S.R.L.[90]

On the same date, the embassy instructed its banker, Direzione Territoriale Italia Centrale, to effect payment by transfer of the said amount of money into the vendor's account. The letter of instruction was signed by Dr Mahalu as ambassador and by his assistant, Grace Martin, as counsellor, and the money was transferred the next day. It is the unexplained amount of EUR2 065 827.60 above the quoted price that was the subject of the charges.

Despite the strong evidence of suspicious payments relating to the transaction, and after a long trial lasting over five years, the accused were acquitted. One in the turning points of the case was when former President Benjamin Mkapa defended the accused, exonerating him and others of any wrongdoing. This was a landmark case, as it was the first time that the former head of state had defended an accused person in court. The PCCB protested the ruling but opted not to pursue it further, as it had given rise to considerable political sensitivities involving a foreign government.

---

89   See the judgment in *Republic vs. Costa Mahalu and others*.
90   Ibid.

Most of the corruption cases have taken inordinately long to prosecute. Suggestions are being made for the amendment of the law to provide the PCCB with full prosecutorial powers or to include provisions in the current law requiring the DPP to act within a prescribed period in matters related to corruption, failing which the PCCB can move forward with the prosecutions concerned.

There have been calls for the establishment an independent corruption court to hear and decide all cases and matters related to corruption. By doing this, Tanzania will have followed Uganda's example, where such courts are already in existence.

I. Conclusion

Generally, Tanzania has made significant progress in establishing a legal and institutional anti-corruption framework. Over the years, the PCCB has evolved into a model African anti-corruption institution in terms of both infrastructure and reporting on international anti-corruption instruments. The bureau is headed by a highly trained lawyer, academic and experienced law enforcement officer, Dr Edward Hosea, as DG. The organisation strives to be a transparent institution and has engaged in research in order to inform its anti-corruption efforts. The weakness of the bureau lies, however, in its inability to translate the elaborate institutional apparatus into a robust, efficient agency capable of tackling corruption. The political economy in which corruption takes place in Tanzania has been a contributing factor. Tanzanian polity is characterised by a 'big man syndrome',[91] whereby those in positions of influence are seen as powerful and are often inclined to flaunt this power with impunity. Political patronage is common and those in positions of influence often use public resources or positions to reward political supporters, and vice versa. Tanzanian social relations encourage corruption, because people expect to receive favours from their relatives in power, and corrupt public and private leaders who amass wealth irrespective of the means are at times celebrated and revered by society as 'successful'. Citizens and corporates have therefore been driven towards embracing corruption. For fear of social and/or political retribution, and becuase of a lack of strong protection mechanisms provided by anti-corruption agencies, they are reluctant to report curruption and testify against suspects.

The institution is limited by law (the PCCA) to operating only on mainland Tanzania, and this affects its overall mandate in tackling corruption in the country, since Zanzibar is covered by another agency (ZACEA). Tanzania therefore has multiple agencies dealing with corruption, and, in practice, coordinating activities can be challenging. The bureau and the DG have no constitutional backing to cushion them against any politically motivated shocks and interference that may arise. The bureau is also vulnerable to political, financial and legal risks. As a consequence of the legal, institutional structure, capacity, financial and political hurdles, the bureau is struggling to meet the expectations of the general public and justify its existence in tackling corruption.

---

91   Hanns Seidel Foundation (2013) IV Pan-African Anti-Corruption Conference: Corruption and Development in Africa, Dar es Salaam, 4–5 June 2013, p. 9.

J. Recommendations

In order to address some of these challenges, the following recommendations are being made:

1. Strengthen the overall legal framework for combating corruption

Generally, Tanzania has a robust legal framework that is well linked with continental and international anti-corruption regimes. The effective implementation of this legal framework is, however, problematic. At least 90% of of 13 526 respondents (households and public officials) interviewed in a PCCB-commissioned study in 2009 believed that poor law enforcement or inadequate punishment of the culprits were factors responsible for corruption.[92] Over a third of respondents interviewed by Transparency International saw no reason for reporting the payment of bribes, because they believed no action would be taken against the culprits.[93] There is therefor a need to address some of the legal lacunae that make enforcement, and the punishment of corruption, difficult. This can be done in the following ways:

- Tanzania should support the adoption of the East African Protocol on Combating Corruption (it has been in draft form for too long).
- The government of Tanzania should urgently enact and pass an access-to-information law (ATI), which was first mooted in 2006. President Kiwete also undertook on 31 October 2013 to have a Bill sent to parliament and gave assurances that an ATI law would be passed by April 2014. In March 2015, this Bill was presented to parliament under a certificate of urgency, but was later withdrawn. Since then, there has been no progress.
- Allocate resources to protect informers and implement witness protection programmes, as per sections 51 and 52, respectively, of the PCCA. The PCCB should advocate for these resources to be available.
- Establish corruption courts to expedite corruption cases. The pioneering case law from these courts could also help in opening up a new frontier in anti-corruption proceedings.
- Appropriate measures are needed to encourage persons who participate, or who have participated, in the commission of an offence established in accordance with the PCCA to supply information useful to competent authorities for investigative and evidentiary purposes and to provide factual, specific help to competent authorities that may contribute to depriving offenders of the proceeds of crime and to recovering such proceeds. Currently, this discretion lies only with the courts.
- Introduce legal reforms that provide for mitigation based on collaboration with anti-corruption agencies. Mitigation of punishment based on collaboration with

---

92 PCCB (2009) *National Governance and Corruption Survey 2009*. FACEIT in association with Dar Consultants. 21 November 2009.
93 Transparency International-Kenya (2013) *East African Bribery Index 2013*. Nairobi, Kenya: TI-Kenya.

law enforcement agencies is currently only the prerogative of the courts. For this to happen, suspects will have to cooperate with law enforcement before they have participated in a criminal act, not afterwards.

- The anti-corruption legal framework in Tanzania should be reformed to allow for plea bargaining and for the signing of treaties catering for plea bargains between Tanzania and other countries. Among other benefits, this will increase intelligence on and knowledge of corruption within and outside Tanzania.

2. Strengthen the PCCB's status (legal framework, appointment, tenure and removal procedures, external oversight, autonomy and independence)

- Reforms are required to ensure that the PCCB is rooted in the Constitution. Currently, it is not a constitutional body and thus its existence is not certain. This constitutional rootedness needs to be matched by gazetting of corruption as a union matter as well.
- There is a need to secure the tenure of the head of the PCCB. The current law does not provide for security of tenure, nor is the position anchored in the Constitution.
- There is a need for an independent, external oversight body to be created. Currently, the PCCB's oversight structures are vague. The law is also silent on this.
- Move the PCCB away from the presidency and ensure that it is free of political interference. This oversight role can be given to parliament or the judiciary.
- Ensure that the new constitution provides a high degree of independence for the PCCB.
- Consider transforming the bureau into an anti-corruption commission with publicly vetted commissioners. This will give it more autonomy and cushion it against possible interference.
- As an anti-corruption agency, the PCCB itself might not be free of corruption. The question therefore arises as to who exercises checks in respect of corrupt conduct of the PCCB as an institution. Related to this issue, it is important to have clarity as to where citizens can report corruption, for example corruption involving senior officials of the PCCB.

3. Strengthen the mandate and interagency collaboration with state and non-state actors and with regional/continental networks

- Extend the jurisdiction and mandate of the PCCB to include Zanzibar, with the ZACEA working as a sub-agency under the PCCB. Having dual or multiple agencies engaged in anti-corruption activities in one country has proven a failure in many countries, like Nigeria and South Africa.
- At the moment, it appears that there is no clarity regarding how the mainland

and Zanzibar work together to monitor and fight corruption, even though the anti-corruption agencies may gain constitutional recognition in the proposed constitution. In the event that corruption is accorded the status of a union matter, it will be important that the institutions involved (the PCCB and the ZACEA) draw up a framework for collaboration that will allow corruption to be addressed as a countrywide issue.

- The mandate of the PCCB to deal with cases needs to be expanded. For example, embezzlement cases under the Penal Code, when sent to the DPP, are referred to the police and are not brought before the PCCB. There have been few cases under the PCCA, because the DPP prefers to deal with cases under the Penal Code.
- There is a need for more interagency collaboration. As with intergovernmental cooperation between the mainland and Zanzibar, there is clearly a challenge regarding interagency cooperation and information sharing. This needs to be improved across the board to avoid the possibility of agencies operating in isolation and undermining the effectiveness of sanctions which are imposed from time to time.
- There is limited interagency collaboration between the PCCB, the FIU, the police and the DPP. According to the PCCB, the need for the DPP's consent presents challenges in practice, because the DPP has a large workload involving all criminal matters, thus leading to delays. Pending receipt of consent, suspects are released on bail. The DPP has assigned special officers to deal with corruption cases. However, there is still a need to enhance the DPP's understanding of handling corruption prosecutions.
- There should be an investigation of the factors that limit efficiency and effectiveness in the cooperation arrangement between the PCCB and DPP. The underlying issues inhibit limit progress in prosecutions should be addressed.
- Increased high-level advocacy against secrecy jurisdictions and complex financial systems which enable corruption to thrive, is needed. The PCCB needs to openly join the global campaign for financial transparency.
- Collaboration with non-state actors, and their active participation in the PCCB's anti-corruption work, should be increased. Currently, this collaboration is not formalised and the level of engagement is erratic.

4. Improve the PCCB's financing, independence and sustainability

In respect of financial independence, it is necessary to ensure that there is sufficient funding of the PCCB to enable it to execute its mandated functions without any delay. Key anti-corruption projects and programmes, like the NACSAP, have been heavily reliant on donor funding, and, consequently, their continuity is not guaranteed. The study recommends that, to the extent possible, the PCCB be fully funded from internal resources to avoid the problems caused by the unreliability of donor financing.

5. Strengthen administration, staff capacity and infrastructure

The PCCB is a well-established institution and, from the available information, it is evident that the capacity of the organisation has been increasing. The number of legal staff has increased and now stands at 80 advocates and 120 legal officers. Nonetheless, the level of experience and the performance of the institution need to be improved. To improve its efficiency, the organisation needs to take the following actions:

- Invest in sophisticated technology to track suspected corrupt transactions and criminals within and outside the country's borders.
- Solicit more onsite assistance from corruption experts on modern ways of combating corruption, including staging 'sting' operations and anti-corruption 'surgical' raids.
- Enlist legal advice on legislative drafting and prosecution from competent individuals and institutions. The PCCB should be staffed with young legal officers and advocates whose experience matches that of the top senior advocates and law firms enlisted by corruption suspects.
- Introduce specialised training in investigative skills and prosecution techniques. Training should involve the judiciary, the DPP, the PCCB and the police. The PCCA is not well understood by judges. Furthermore, understanding complex corruption and offences like sexual corruption, trading in influence, and determining the level of guilt, is sometimes a challenge for some judicial officers.
- The PCCB needs to use the available studies and reports on corruption to mount anti-corruption operations, for example sting operations, laying traps, and surveillance, against corruption-prone departments and public-service points.
- Invest in more community sensitisation about the impact of corruption on social-service delivery and on the overall development of communities and the entire country. Sharing vivid examples of corruption cases and their impact could be vital in enlisting more support from the public.
- Sharing of good practices and model legislation from other countries can improve the organisation's performance.
- Communicate regularly with the public regarding the bureau's performance and practically demonstrate this with actual figures on arrests and prosecutions conducted during a particular period (either on a monthly or bimonthly basis) across the country. The level of public interface with the agency is limited.
- Improve the quality data collection relating to corruption cases. So far, statistics have been collected and presented at aggregate level, and these need to be disaggregated by type of corruption offence and possibly by sector.
- The PCCB should establish and implement a functional feedback mechanism capable of providing the public with regular (monthly or quarterly) on what happens to their tip-offs and updates on the PCCB's investigative and prosecutorial activities, etc. The PCCB needs to be more innovative in this regard.

ANNEX I: PCCB's organogram, 2014

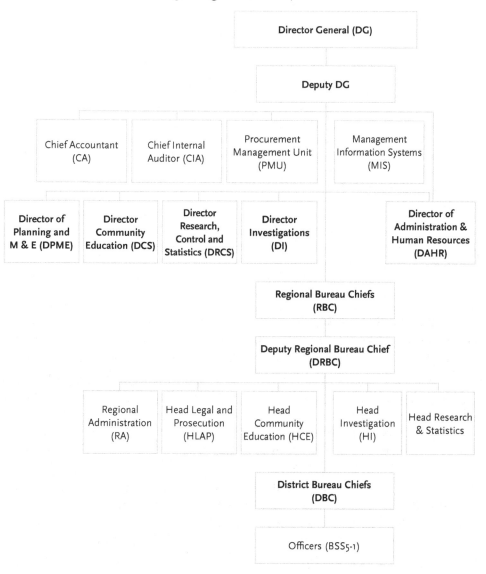

4

Uganda

A. Executive summary

The elimination of corruption and abuse of office featured prominently in the ten-point programme formulated by the incumbent National Resistance Movement (NRM) during the five-year guerrilla war that eventually ushered the regime into power in 1986. Unfortunately, the fight against corruption is mostly confined to political speeches and, to some extent, statute books.

Uganda signed and ratified the United Nations Convention against Corruption (UNCAC) on 9 December 2003 and 9 September 2004, respectively. Uganda is also a state party to the African Union Convention on Preventing and Combating Corruption (AU Convention). The Constitution of the Republic of Uganda and the National Objectives and Directive Principles of State Policy (NODPSP) enjoin the state to adopt all lawful means to eradicate corruption and abuse of power. The Constitution also empowers the Inspectorate of Government (IG) to enforce the Leadership Code of Conduct and the Anti-Corruption Act of 2009. The 2002 Inspectorate of Government Act operationalises the constitutional provisions on the establishment of the IG. The law guarantees the independence of the IG in more specific terms under article 227 of the Constitution and section 10 of the Inspectorate of Government Act. The IG is required to submit a report to parliament every six months. Article 299 of the Constitution provides that the IG must have an independent budget appropriated by parliament and controlled by the inspectorate. This relative independence is, however, threatened by the conflicting responsibility of parliament for reappointing the inspector general of government (IGG) and deputy inspectors general (DIG), with parliament's responsibility for ensuring accountability among parliamentarians. The IGG, assisted by the DIG, is appointed by the president but can only be removed by a tribunal on the recommendation of parliament, thus ensuring the relative independence of the IGG.

The IG has both investigative and prosecutorial powers. It can also seize assets found to have been corruptly acquired.

The IG has an independent budget appropriated by parliament that it controls, though the IG has deemed the current budgetary allocations to be inadequate.

The IG has been successful in creating an environment that reduces corruption. Its prosecution strategy appears to focus on junior- or mid-level civil servants. However, the tone of the president has been ambivalent, leading to the perception that the government uses the IG's office to serve political interests.

This report recommends expediting the proposed amendments to the 2009 Anti-Corruption Act that provide for mandatory confiscation of the property of persons convicted of corruption and its related offences. It also recommends that the investigative and prosecutorial roles of the IGG and director of public prosecutions (DPP) be streamlined under the law to avoid the current overlaps and duplication that strain limited resources.

The IG's focus on low- and mid-level civil servants seems to favour corrupt high-ranking civil servants and those with political clout. It is important that the IG treat all cases equally and expeditiously. This may be difficult considering Uganda's political reality.

B. Introduction

The elimination of corruption and abuse of office featured prominently in the ten-point programme formulated by the incumbent National Resistance Movement (NRM) during the five-year guerrilla war that eventually ushered the regime into power in 1986. The inclusion of corruption on the list of urgent issues that the new government would tackle reflected a strong initial commitment on the part of the NRM to end corruption and to promote accountability. Indeed, this commitment flourished during the first few years of the NRM's rule. The new government, among other things, enacted anti-corruption legislation in the first two years after coming into power. Under the law, the Office of the Inspector General of Government (IGG) was established to investigate instances of corruption, which was an important step in the fight against corruption at the time.

Unfortunately, after a few years in power, the NRM's strong stance against corruption began to weaken and, at the time of writing, there is still lack of political will to tackle corruption decisively. The fight against corruption has, for the most part, been confined to political speeches and a number of statutes that, for a number of reasons explored in this chapter, have been rendered dysfunctional. This soft approach has caused corruption to thrive, and, consequently, Uganda has seen a tremendous increase in the number of corruption cases, including petty corruption, grand corruption, political corruption, bribery, nepotism, and abuse of office.

C. State of corruption

Over the last decade, Uganda has been rocked by grand-corruption scandals involving the loss of staggering amounts of public funds. In 2007, for instance, substantial amounts of money were lost through the procurement of cars and other items required for the Commonwealth Heads of Government Meeting (CHOGM). At the end of 2006, in excess of USD37 million intended for the treatment of malaria, HIV/Aids and tuberculosis was confirmed unaccounted for. Earlier in the same year, over USD890 000 (UGX1.6 billion) in funds earmarked by the Global Alliance for Vaccines and Immunisation (GAVI) was lost. Three government ministers, including Jim Muhwezi, Mike Mukula and Dr Alex Kamugisha, were implicated in the scandal. In 2011, over USD1.7 million was lost in a botched purchase of 70 000 bicycles for members of local council committees across the country. In 2012, officials in the Office of the Prime Minister were alleged to have stolen close to EUR12 intended for the reconstruction of war-ravaged areas in northern Uganda and some eastern parts of the country. In the same year, there occurred outright theft of USD65 million (UGX169 billion) in pension funds intended for the compensation of 1 018 former workers of the East African Community.

While the scale of theft of public resources illustrated above is worrisome, these cases represent only a small proportion of the grand-corruption cases that have come to light over the past decade. According to the Transparency International Corruption Perceptions Index (CPI), Uganda ranked 140 out of 177 countries in 2013 in terms of corruption. In 2012, the country ranked 130 out of 176 countries, while in 2011 it ranked 143 out of 183 countries. The 2012 East African Bribery index (EABI) ranked Uganda as the worst among the five East African countries in terms of bribery.

In 2012, a group of civil-society organisations declared a week of national mourning and launched several anti-corruption activities in protest against the levels of corruption and apparent government reluctance to decisively tackle it. Under the umbrella of the Black Monday Movement (BMM), civil-society groups demanded the immediate resignation of those implicated in corruption and urgent intervention by the government to end corruption. The activists donned black outfits as a sign of mourning the loss of public funds and accountability. The group also issued flyers to the public bearing anti-corruption messages.

In its response, the Ugandan government deployed armed police and anti-riot equipment and arrested a number of activists for distributing what was referred to as 'harmful propaganda'. To date, the BMM is not allowed to freely mobilise and distribute anti-corruption materials anywhere in the country.

Indeed, if the proposed legal framework for non-governmental organisations (NGOs) is implemented, there is a fear that anti-corruption efforts will be stifled further due to the restrictive operational environment that the law seeks to introduce. This, again, demonstrates the state's reluctance to join hands with anti-corruption activists to end corruption once and for all.

The politics of corruption

The use of money to influence election processes and outcomes is a reality in Uganda. In the 2001 and 2006 elections, bribery of voters was cited through the myriad of election petitions brought before court, for example: (1) *Rtd. Col. Dr Kizza Besigye vs. President Yoweri Museveni and the Electoral Commission*, Presidential Election Petition No. 1 of 2006; (2) *Abdu Katuntu vs. Ali Kirunda Kivejinja and the Electoral Commission*, Electoral Petition No. 7 of 2006, High Court of Uganda; and (3) *James Garuga Musinguzi vs. Amama Mbabazi and the Electoral Commission*, Electoral Petition No. 5 of 2001, High Court of Uganda.

According to a 2010 report by Afrimap, the pervasive use of money to decide elections has become an entrenched norm in Uganda. Between November and December 2010, the DEM Group conducted research in 20 districts in all regions of Uganda which confirmed that vote-buying happens at all levels of elective political positions and in every region.

The same report laments that incumbent candidates readily use their access to state resources to gain an unfair advantage when running for re-election. This includes cash payments from the state treasury, the use of state-owned property and vehicles, as well as the fulfilment of campaign pledges during the campaign period. Voters have given up on their elected officials fulfilling campaign promises and seek to extract as much benefit as they can around the campaign period.

D. Civil society, donors and media engagement

The Inspectorate of Government (IG) maintains a healthy relationship with civil society and the media. For example, it has in the recent past signed a memorandum of understanding (MoU) with the Uganda Debt Network to implement the social-accountability and community-monitoring (SACM) activity of the transparency, accountability and anti-corruption component of the Second Northern Uganda Social Action Fund (NUSAF II). Under the MoU, the Uganda Debt Network is working with the IG to build the capacity of communities to monitor government-funded projects and thus enhance transparency and accountability. In May 2014, community monitors and regional managers from various community monitoring groups were trained in anti-corruption reporting mechanisms. In the same spirit, the IG and the media enjoy a cordial relationship that has resulted in coverage of the activities of the IG and in the reporting of abuses of office and corruption in the media. Recently, the media reported on corruption and abuses of office at the Uganda National Roads Authority, a case in which a contract to construct a road (the Mukono-Katosi road) was irregularly awarded to a non-existent entity. At the time of writing, this matter is being investigated by the IG.

The IG does not have prominent relationships with private-sector organisations. This may be attributed to the fact that the IG is interested in corruption and abuses of office in public bodies. This mandate is constraining, especially in cases where corrupt acts involve public officers conniving with private-sector actors.

E. Commitment to international conventions

Uganda is party to a number of regional and international anti-corruption conventions, declarations and initiatives. The country signed and ratified the United Nations Convention against Corruption (UNCAC) on 9 December 2003 and 9 September 2004, respectively. Uganda is also a state party to the African Union Convention on Preventing and Combating Corruption (AU Convention). These two conventions reflect global and regional consensus on corruption and thus create a number of obligations for states parties like Uganda. States parties are required to develop anti-corruption prevention policies, practices, and bodies. In addition, states are obligated to establish codes of conduct for their public officials and to put in place appropriate systems for public procurement that promote, among other things, competition and transparency. These are critical in the fight against, and eventual defeat, of corruption. As stated above, regional and international legal frameworks greatly influence domestic legal frameworks, and this holds true for Uganda.

Domestication of international conventions

Uganda has domesticated the UNCAC and AU Convention through various pieces of legislation and institutions elaborated on herein.

F. Legal framework for preventing and combating corruption

The Constitution of the Republic of Uganda

At national level, the commitment to end corruption is reflected in the 1995 Constitution of Uganda. According to principle XXVI of the National Objectives and Directive Principles of State Policy (NODPSP), the state is enjoined to adopt all lawful means to eradicate corruption and abuse of power. Initially, there was considerable debate as to whether the NODPSP should be enforced at the same level as other provisions of the Constitution. The 2005 constitutional amendment settled this question; hence the NODPSP is now enforceable as part of the Constitution. This means that principle XXVI is as binding on the state as if it had been contained in the main articles of the Constitution.

The duty to eliminate corruption and abuses of authority is also reflected in a number of other constitutional provisions, including those that establish the Office of the IG. Under chapter 13, the IG has several functions, key of which is the mandate to 'eliminate and foster the elimination of corruption, abuse of authority and public office'. In order to fulfil this function, the IG is given special powers to investigate, arrest and prosecute in cases involving corruption and abuses of public office.

The Constitution empowers the IG to enforce the Leadership Code of Conduct, which is contained in the Leadership Code Act enacted by parliament in accordance with article 233 of the Constitution. Under the Leadership Code of Conduct, specified officers are obligated to declare their incomes, assets and liabilities. The code also prohibits certain conduct likely to encourage corruption and/or compromise values of honesty and impartiality.

The Constitution also confers an express duty on every citizen to combat corruption and the misuse or wastage of public property. It is worth noting that corruption in its most common form involves a public official granting favours in exchange for a reward, or rewards, from members of the public. Willingness on the part of the public is therefore essential for corruption to thrive. If citizens embrace their constitutional duty to combat corruption, this could go a long way towards ridding society of corruption.

The Anti-Corruption Act

The principal piece of legislation dealing with preventing and combating corruption is the Anti-Corruption Act of 2009. This law sets out to, among other things, repeal and replace the Prevention of Corruption Act of 1970, prevent corruption in the public and private sectors, and amend the Penal Code Act and the Leadership Code Act. The Anti-Corruption Act consolidates corruption and all other related offences in one text. The Act also confers special powers on the IGG and the director of public prosecutions (DPP) to investigate and prosecute corruption cases. In essence, the IGG and the DPP enjoy equal powers in the investigation and prosecution of the offence of corruption and related offences. While this is seemingly positive, there are concerns that this equality may lead to conflict between the two offices and to possible acrimony when there is a failure to duly investigate and prosecute particular cases. The DPP and the IGG also operate with extremely limited resources, and the duplication of duties is therefore likely to lead to wastage of these already meagre resources.

The Anti-Corruption Act introduces a broader definition of corruption and expands on the scope of offences previously contained in the Prevention of Corruption Act and the Penal Code Act. It introduces new offences such as influence-peddling, conflict of interest, sectarianism, and nepotism, to mention but a few. All of these were not included in the Prevention of Corruption Act and the Penal Code Act. The offences of embezzlement, false accounting, abuse of office, and impersonation of public officials, which were previously contained in the Penal Code Act, have been retained. The only challenge as regards this law is that some of the offences – such as abuse of office and causing financial loss – are overly broadly defined, which makes it difficult for prosecutors to sustain charges. It is proposed that these offences be defined with more specificity, as is the case under international and regional treaties on combating corruption.

These reforms in the law should be taken together with current proposals to amend the Anti-Corruption Act in order to allow for confiscation of properties belonging to persons convicted of corruption and related offences.

The Leadership Code Act

Besides the Anti-Corruption Act, there are several other laws that deal with corruption. The Leadership Code Act mentioned above is one of these. This law puts in place a code and enjoins specified officers to declare their assets every two years. Failure to comply with this provision amounts to a breach of the code and attracts a penalty. In 2005, the

Constitution was amended to provide for the establishment of a special tribunal that would be responsible for enforcement of the Leadership Code. To date, members of this tribunal have not been appointed, which is a clear demonstration of the lack of political will to decisively tackle corruption.

The Inspectorate of Government Act
The Inspectorate of Government Act of 2002 operationalises the constitutional provisions on the establishment of the IG. It spells out the appointment procedures, as well as the constitution, powers, and functions of the inspectorate, and other related matters.

The Anti-Money Laundering Act
The recently enacted Anti-Money Laundering Act is yet another piece of legislation that, when fully enforced, will help in the efforts to curb corruption. The Act makes it an offence to accumulate wealth through illegitimate means and imposes responsibilities and sanctions on institutions and persons likely to be used in the accumulation of such wealth. The Act also provides for the seizure, freezing and forfeiture of assets obtained through money laundering. In addition, the law provides for international cooperation in the investigation and prosecution of money-laundering activities.

Other laws that contain anti-corruption provisions include the Access to Information Act, 2005; the Whistle Blower Protection Act, 2010; and the Public Procurement and Disposal of Public Assets Act, 2013. Access to information, protection of whistle-blowers, and open procurement are key tenets in the fight against corruption to the extent that they promote transparency, which, in turn, promotes accountability.

G. The Inspectorate of Government
The IG is established under chapter 13 of the Constitution of the Republic of Uganda. The IG is constituted by the IGG and a number of DIG as parliament may legally prescribe. In 2002, parliament enacted the Inspectorate of Government Act which, among other things, prescribed the number of DIG as two. The main objective of the Act is to give effect to provisions of the Constitution pertaining to the IG. The law in effect reiterates the constitutional provisions on the establishment of the IG and expands on the scope of the IG's functions. In terms of jurisdiction, the IG covers officers and leaders employed in the public service and other such institutions, organisations and enterprises as parliament may by law prescribe. The categories of individuals and institutions over whom the IG exercises jurisdiction are included in the Inspectorate of Government Act.

Independence
The law guarantees the independence of the IG in more specific terms in article 227 of the Constitution and section 10 of the Inspectorate of Government Act. In terms of these

provisions, the IG is not subject to the direction or control of any person or authority in the performance of its functions and is only responsible to parliament.

As part of its responsibilities, the IG is required to submit a report to parliament every six months. The report must outline its performance and make necessary recommendations. The report must also contain any other information that parliament may require. On receipt of the report, the speaker of parliament is required to place the report before parliament within 30 days. Parliament may then take any action as it deems appropriate. An additional copy of the report is required to be forwarded to the president and to a local government authority to which any of the matters in the report relate.

Article 299 of the Constitution provides that the IG must have an independent budget appropriated by parliament and controlled by the inspectorate. This provision is restated in section 31(1) of the Inspectorate of Government Act. The secretary of the IG is required to prepare and submit the IG's annual budget to parliament. Once approved, the requested monies are charged to the consolidated fund.

The IGG and the DIG are appointed by the president, but may only be removed from office on recommendation of a special tribunal formed by parliament. Therefore, they enjoy relative security of tenure. Further guarantees of independence are contained in provisions pertaining to the appointment and removal of the IGG and the DIG.

This relative independence is, however, threatened by conflict between parliament's responsibility to reappoint the IGG and the DIG, on the one hand, and the IGG's responsibility for ensuring accountability among parliamentarians, on the other. Members of parliament (MPs) are among the public officers required by the Leadership Code Act to declare their wealth and assets. In 2006, the IGG successfully petitioned for the removal of an MP representing Lubaga North on account of his failure to declare his wealth and assets as per the law. However, the same MP made it back to parliament in 2011. A number of ministers have also been investigated and prosecuted by the IGG over the past few years. It is difficult for parliamentarians who have been investigated and prosecuted to exercise objectivity and impartiality in relation to the reappointment of the IGG and his or her deputies. For this reason, it is proposed that the IGG only be appointed for one non-renewable term of office. In this way, the IGG would exercise the mandate of the office without having to be concerned, at the time of reappointment, about having to face the same officials he or she investigated in the past.

Stability of the inspectorate
The IG has not experienced any major destabilisation since its inception.

IG staff

As mentioned above, the IG is headed by the IGG and is assisted by two DIG, all of whom are appointed by the president of the Republic of Uganda, and at least one of whom must be qualified for appointment as a judge of the high court of Uganda.

Article 223 of the 1995 Constitution of the Republic of Uganda and section 3 of the

2002 Inspectorate of Government Act set out the appointment procedures. All three presidential appointees are, with the approval of parliament, granted terms of four years and are eligible for reappointment only once. While appointed, they cannot hold any other office of emolument in the public service.

To be eligible for these offices, a person must be a Ugandan citizen of high moral character and proven integrity, must have considerable experience, and must have demonstrated competence. To ensure that the appointed person meets these required standards, thorough investigations are conducted into his or her background, character and previous work track record before parliament approves the presidential appointment. In addition, any member of the public who has information relevant to the appointee's character, experience or integrity is allowed to submit this to the Parliamentary Appointments Committee for its consideration as part of the approval process.

If the IGG or a DIG is an MP, a member of a local-government council, or a member of the executive of a political party or organisation, he or she will be required to resign from such office before assuming his or her duties. Moreover, he or she must take, and subscribe to, an oath administered by the president of the Republic of Uganda.

The current IGG is a judge and she is assisted by the two DIG.

The IG has a secretary, who is also the accounting officer appointed by the president on the advice of the Public Service Commission and who heads the Department of Finance and Administration. The secretary holds office on such terms and conditions as are applicable to a permanent secretary and must be a person qualified to be appointed to the Office of Permanent Secretary.

For purposes of carrying out its functions and realising its objectives, the IG is structured as a department, six directorates and two divisions.

All members of the IG, with the exception of the secretary, are appointed by an Appointments Board established in terms of section 7 of the 2002 Inspectorate of Government Act, and on such terms and conditions as the board determines.

The board consists of: the IGG as its chairperson; the two DIG; the secretary of the IG; the chairperson of the Public Service Commission, or a member of that commission authorised by the chairperson in writing; the permanent secretary of the ministry responsible for the public service; and two other members appointed by the president, one of whom must be a woman.

The IG staff are appointed on the basis of their integrity and competence and are usually appointed in terms of a four-year renewable contract, although some may serve a shorter term, depending on the decision of the Appointments Board. The IG can likewise engage the services of, or work in consultation with, professional or technical experts to enhance its performance. The IG is free to recruit based on its identified needs. Vacancies are advertised in the press for the available staff positions. Interviews are held by the Appointments Board responsible for recruitment.

Termination of a contract of appointment usually follows investigation and an opportunity to be heard by the Appointments Board. In addition, there is a human resource manual that applies to all members of the IG, and which incorporates ethical standards and regulations that control conflicts of interest. This manual is provided for under the law, which tends to improve its enforcement. In order to ensure that the manual keeps up to date with the needs of the inspectorate, it is periodically reviewed by a crosscutting team.

The law guarantees members of the IG immunity against civil and criminal proceedings in respect of acts undertaken in the course of their duties and in good faith. Similarly, such officers cannot be compelled to testify before any court or tribunal regarding any information received by them in the course of exercising their assigned functions.

The law does not provide for an acting IGG in the event of the suspension, dismissal, resignation, retirement or death of the incumbent. However, the Ugandan Constitutional Court has previously ruled that a DIG, acting as the IGG, derives the mandate to run the IG from his or her substantive appointment as DIGG, and that the designation IGG is only administrative. Consequently, procedures for the recruitment and termination of staff of the IG are generally transparent.

The Directorate of Education is responsible for the training of staff, and plans for such training. A training plan for staff is drawn up each year and attendees are chosen through their line directorates or units. The head of the directorate concerned is required to exercise fairness in nomination which staff members will attend training, and must take into consideration the needs of the various members.

The IG has an independent budget appropriated by parliament and controlled by the inspectorate. The budget covers, among other things, the salaries and allowances of the secretary and other IG staff. The budget is prepared annually by the secretary and, on approval by the IG, is submitted to parliament for its approval under article 229 of the Constitution.

Security of tenure

Under article 224 of the Constitution of the Republic of Uganda and section 5 of the Inspectorate of Government Act, 2002, the IGG or DIG can only be removed from office by the president on the recommendation of a special tribunal constituted by parliament. The basis for removal includes:

- The inability to perform the functions of his or her office arising from infirmity of body or mind;
- Misconduct, misbehaviour, or conduct unbecoming of the holder of the office; and
- Incompetence.

The special tribunal consists of a justice of the supreme court as its chairperson and two other persons appointed by parliament.

Capacity

The IG currently has staff located in the head office in Kampala, and in 16 regional offices strategically spread out across all the regions of the country.

IG staff members are trained by way of relevant training programmes and study tours, both at individual and group level, in order to equip them with the knowledge, skills and attitudes to optimise their performance. These programmes are mainly undertaken in-country owing to resource considerations, although, on occasion staff, have participated in training programmes abroad. The range of training has included:

- Report-writing (for senior staff);
- Practical and technical issues relating to whistle-blowing and witness protection;
- Harmonisation of laws governing anti-corruption authorities;
- Asset recovery;
- Development of web applications using open-source tools;
- Prosecution of corruption and related crime; and
- Illicit financial flows.

Remuneration

The remuneration of staff has recently been increased, although IG employees opined that their salary levels should at least be on the same levels as those of employees in the Office of the Auditor General.

Investigative and prosecutorial powers

The inspectorate is constitutionally mandated to eliminate corruption, promote and foster the rule of law and principles of natural justice in public offices, and enforce the Leadership Code. The IG is also mandated to sensitise and educate the public on the values of constitutionalism and civic responsibility. This function is implemented through the Directorate of Education and the Directorate of Prevention of Corruption.

Under article 230, the Constitution confers on the IG the power 'to investigate, cause investigation, arrest, cause arrest, prosecute or cause prosecution in respect of cases involving corruption, abuse of authority or of public office'. Further, the IG does not require the consent or approval of any person or authority to prosecute, or to discontinue proceedings instituted by it.

Under section 24 of the Act, a complaint or allegation made to the IG may be made by an individual or by any body of persons, whether corporate or not, must be treated with strict confidentiality, and must be addressed to the IG. If a prisoner or an employee in a public office makes an allegation or complaint to the IG, such allegation or complaint must not be made through, or subject to the scrutiny of, prison officials or the immediate supervisor or employer, as the case may be.

A complaint or allegation made to the inspectorate is made in writing by the complainant, or by his or her legal representative, and is addressed to the IG, except where the complainant cannot write, in which case the inspectorate is required to translate the oral complaint into writing and to ensure that it is signed by the complainant or bears his or her thumbprint.

In all cases prosecuted by the IGG, he or she must afford the same rights of appeal as afforded by the director of public prosecutions.

The IGG or DIG must sanction any complaint before it is investigated. Generally, the guiding principles for making such a decision include: whether the IG has jurisdiction; whether alternative remedies have been explored, or if there is justification for referring the matter to the IG; and whether another competent authority is already handling the matter.

In the implementation of the anti-corruption function, the inspectorate carries out investigations where the commission of any offence under the 2009 Anti-Corruption Act or the Leadership Code Act is alleged. Where the subject of an investigation is found to have committed an offence, he or she may be arrested and prosecuted. Disciplinary action varies from warnings, to dismissal, to recovery of monies lost or embezzled. The IG may also confiscate the assets of a public officer where investigations establish them to have been acquired through corrupt means.

The inspectorate does not, however, have the power to question or review:

- The decision of any court of law or of any judicial officer in the exercise of his or her judicial functions;
- The decision of any tribunal established by law in the exercise of its functions;
- Any civil matter that is before court at the commencement of the inspectorate's investigations; or
- Any matter relating to the exercise of the prerogative of mercy or review or investigation that has been certified by the president as likely to either be prejudicial to the security, defence or international relations of Uganda or to involve the disclosure of proceedings and deliberations of the cabinet, or a committee of cabinet, relating to matters of a secret or confidential nature that would be injurious to the public interest.

Article 232 of the Constitution of the Republic of Uganda mandates parliament to make laws to give effect to the provisions in the Constitution regarding the IG. The major law in this respect has been the Inspectorate of Government Act. Parliament also introduced a Leadership Code of Conduct which requires specified officers to declare their incomes, assets and liabilities from time to time, as well as how they acquired or incurred them. The IG has, however, complained of loopholes in the existing legal framework, such as the absence of a leadership code tribunal as prescribed under chapter 14 of the Constitution, and the absence of regulations to establish rules of procedure under the Inspectorate of Government Act and the 2002 Leadership Code Act. Such gaps affect the enforcement of the IG's recommendations in respect of leaders who are found to be in breach of the Leadership Code of Conduct. Without a leadership code tribunal, the IG cannot effectively implement its mandate of enforcing the Leadership Code of Conduct. According to the IG report to parliament for July to December 2013, leaders must declare their assets and liabilities as required by law, but, because of the absence of a tribunal, it is difficult for the IG to take any action against those who fail to comply with this requirement, or who underreport their wealth.

Under article 231 of the Constitution, the IG is required to submit a report to parliament at least once every six months on the performance of its functions, and which further makes recommendations that the office considers necessary for the efficient performance of public institutions. The report is also meant to provide any other information that parliament may require.

The speaker of parliament must place before parliament any report within 30 days after it has been submitted, if parliament is in session, or within 30 days after the commencement of its next session, if it is not in session. On receipt of a report, parliament may take, or cause to be taken, such action as it may consider appropriate.

Article 231(5) of the Constitution provides for parliament to debate IG reports and make recommendations on the issues raised. However, at the time of writing of this report, the IG had allegedly not received any feedback from parliament and the executive on the reports issued, which feedback it requires for improved performance.

The police can investigate cases of corruption or fraud. The IG further collaborates with the police when necessary in order to recover assets acquired by public officers by corrupt means.

The dilemma is that the Ugandan police force is one of the most corrupt public institutions in the country according to the IG's report to parliament for July to December 2013. This specific report states that complaints against the Ugandan police constituted 7.7% of the total complaints received for the period. The nature of complaints against the police include mishandling of cases, bribery, abuse of office, and delays in service delivery. The Ugandan police force is thus the most bribery-prone of the country's institutions, largely because bribery is either demanded by police officers or is offered by people seeking services from them. The IG has recommended regularly transferring police officers, in addition to capacity building of the Uganda Police Professional Standards Unit, in order to curb corruption within the force. Despite this trend, investigation of corrupt practices has remained a responsibility shared by the IG and the police. Because corruption involves criminal acts, the police force has an anti-corruption department that investigates corruption cases involving public officials. According to the IG's Fourth Annual Report on Tracking Corruption Trends in Uganda: Using the Data Tracking Mechanism,[94] the number of corruption cases reported to the police increased from 46 in 2008 and 95 in 2009 to 413 in 2013, and the police have played an important role in working hand in hand with the IG to curb corruption among public officials.

As a policy, the DPP, the IGG and the High Court of Uganda (Anti-Corruption Division) dispose of cases within four months of their opening. However, appeals, constitutional petitions or references, and applications filed in both the Constitutional Court and the Supreme Court often lead to the delayed conclusion of cases. Owing to these delays, the IG was only able to conclude 32 out of 145 prosecutions in 2013 (a decrease from 86 out of 168 cases in 2012) according to the December 2013 report to parliament.

There are other institutions, such as the auditor general, whose functions relate to detecting financial irregularities or malpractices. Another example is the DPP, who can

---

94   See http://www.igg.go.ug/publications/.

prosecute any criminal cases, including those related to corruption. When article 230 of the Constitution provides that the inspectorate has the power to cause investigation, or to cause prosecution, of cases involving corruption, it has all these institutions in mind for collaborative purposes.

Articles 226 and 227 of the Constitution accord the IG areas of authority and independence. The jurisdiction of the inspectorate covers officers or leaders, whether employed in the public service or not, and also such institutions, organisations or enterprises as parliament may prescribe by law. These include the cabinet, parliament itself, courts of law, central and local governments, and statutory corporations, among others.

The office is independent in the performance of its functions and is only responsible to parliament and the president. The IG reports to parliament by submitting biannual reports detailing its activities and performance of mandated functions, as well as making recommendations on how it can be assisted to be more efficient in carrying out its duties. The IG is also required to send a copy of the report to the president.

The inspectorate has the power to call for and carry out investigations. It can also enter and inspect the premises or property of any department of government, person or authority, and, when necessary, examine and retain any document or item found on the premises in connection with the case being investigated.

The IGG, the DIG or any other officer or person authorised by the IG or DIG may, in the performance of their functions, search any person and retain any document or item in connection with the matter being investigated. Additionally, they have access to all books, returns, reports and other documents relating to the work in any public office, and, at any time, they have access to, and are able to search, the premises of any public office, or of any vessel, aircraft or other vehicles, if there is reason to suspect that property corruptly or otherwise unlawfully acquired has been placed, deposited or concealed in it.

For the purpose of exercising his or her powers of access and search, the IGG, the DIG or any other officer or person authorised for the purpose may use such reasonable force as may be necessary in the circumstances and may be accompanied or assisted by such other law enforcement officers as he or she considers necessary to assist him or her to enter into or upon the premises, vessel, aircraft or vehicle, as the case may be.

Under section 14, either the IGG or the DIG may sign an order authorising an officer of the inspectorate – or any other competent person under the control of the inspectorate – to investigate any bank account, purchase account, share account, expense account or any other account, any safe or deposit box in a bank, or any transaction for the purposes of the Act. Such order may direct the suspension of all operations in respect of the account against the holder of the account or any other person, or the stopping of any transaction subject to such conditions as the IGG or DIGG may specify. According to the Fourth Annual Report on Tracking Corruption Trends in Uganda: Using the Data Tracking Mechanism, the IG recovered over UGX1.1 billion out of nearly 5.5 billion recommended for recovery in 2013.

The IG does not investigate the private sector, as the Constitution only mandates it to investigate public office and authorities. The police force has an economic crimes department that investigates corruption practices involving private persons and companies, and collects data on these practices.

Public-feedback mechanism and witness protection

The inspectorate is required to protect the identity of any person who provides information. Further, an informant may be rewarded for their information and paid an amount of 5% of the money recovered consequent to revealing his or her information to the inspectorate. Anyone who unlawfully discloses the identity of an informer or victimises a person for giving information to, or assisting, the inspectorate can be imprisoned for up to two years or fined up to one hundred currency points, or both.

The mechanism by which complainants receive feedback depends on the nature of the complaint. In complaints of an ombudsman/maladministration nature, the complainants are given a number through which they can track the complaint. They also receive feedback orally and in writing at the closing of the complaint, and upon the action taken after a report is issued.

If a complaint is deemed to be corruption-related, the feedback is more guarded, given that it calls for a full-scale investigation. However, at the close of the complaint, the complainant will receive feedback in writing regarding the findings and the action taken. It is worth noting that not all corruption-related complaints involve feedback. This is because each case depends on how the matter has been concluded, and on the discretion of the IGG or DIG.

Financial resources

Planning in respect of the IG's financial resources is undertaken by the secretary to the inspectorate, who is responsible for the annual budget. On approval by the inspectorate, the budget is submitted to parliament. Under the Constitution of the Republic of Uganda, the inspectorate controls an independent budget appropriated by parliament. Often, the financial resources allocated are insufficient to support the requirements of the IG. For example, it was difficult to obtain a budgetary increment for the financial year 2014/2015, despite growing resource needs. For the financial year 2014/2015, statutory salaries had a possible funding variance of over UGX1.5 billion, equivalent to USD596 766.

The budget of Uganda for the financial year 2014/2015 was approximately USD5 billion, equivalent to roughly UGX15 000 billion. The Ministry of Finance, Planning and Economic Development allocated the IG approximately USD11 481 300, thereby creating a funding variance of about USD1 701 538. By contrast, the auditor general's report alone was allocated USD12 443 572 to be paid to contractors in 2013.

Cognisant of financing challenges, the law permits the IG's office to receive grants and donations to help it perform its duties. Bilateral donor support from countries like Denmark (Danida) and the United Kingdom (DFID), and from the World Bank, have supported the IG's office in Uganda and have involved both technical and financial support. Although donor support was suspended in the recent past, donor support has now resumed, albeit in a diminished amount. In 2011, external funding amounted to USD756 923, while, in 2013, it fell to USD719 230. The decline in funding may be attributed to the general aid cuts that have been effected due to the corruption scandals in Uganda.

Table 4.1: Budget summary for allocated budget, government allocation, and donor (external) allocation for the period 2011–2014.

Allocation	Category of allocation	FY 2011/2012		FY 2012/2013		FY 2013/2014 (July–December)	
		Approved budget	Outturn	Approved budget	Outturn	Approved budget	Outturn
Recurrent	Wage	9.899 USD3 807 307	9.899 USD3 807 307	13.18 USD5 069 230	12.1 USD4 653 846	15.18 USD5 838 461	7.628 USD2 933 846
	Non-wage	12.161 USD4 677 307	13.049 USD5 018 846	12.16 USD4 676 923	12.17 USD4 680 769	15.448 USD5 941 538	8.845 USD3 401 923
Development	Ugandan government	1.96 USD753 846	1.891 USD727 307	2.96 USD1 138 461	2.39 USD919 230	2.931 USD1 127 307	1.821 USD700 384
	External financing	1.968 USD756 923	1.968 USD756 923	1.784 USD686 153	1.784 USD686 153	1.87 USD719 230	0.935 USD359 615
Total		25.988 USD9 995 384	26.807 USD10 310 384	30.084 USD11 570 769	28.444 USD10 940 000	35.429 USD13 626 538	19.229 USD7 395 769

The funds allocated to the IG are available to the entity in good time; thus, the challenge is not the period within which funds are disbursed to the entity but rather the amount that is allocated, as discussed above. Once the funds have been allocated, the inspectorate enjoys managerial autonomy through an elaborate governance structure. The funds and the budget are effectively managed by the secretary to the inspectorate. The absorption capacity of the IG varies each financial year and is, in many cases, informed by the programmes and work plan proposed for a particular financial year. That said, it appears that the absorption capacity of the IG is good, as most of the funds allocated are spent. In some cases, the inspectorate has received more funds from donors than anticipated; such funds have then been used to meet the funding gap. No cases of overexpenditure have been reported.

Rules of financial transparency are prepared and applied within the inspectorate to prevent mismanagement of funds and abuse of power. These rules are informed by the IG's values, which include integrity. Members of staff at the IG's office are expected to be transparent in all actions and to be accountable to all stakeholders. In addition to the above values, the inspectorate has internal safeguards to protect its resources. The senior principal inspectorate officer, who reports directly to the IG, ensures transparency and accountability among staff of the inspectorate. This is done through investigating, detecting and curtailing corruption. The senior principal inspectorate officer also vets new recruits. Further, such officer works under the information and internal inspection unit. The external checks are performed by the Office of the Auditor General and, where appropriate, sanctions are imposed. These procedures highlight the independence of the inspectorate, as it is audited like all other independent government bodies.

Figure 4.1: Comparison of the proportion of government funding versus external funding of the IG

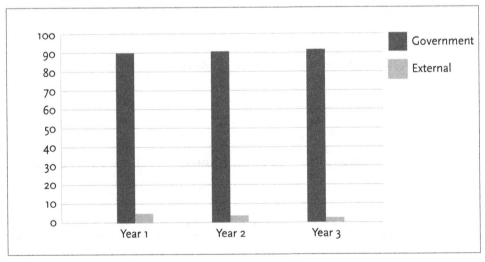

Table 4.2 Budget allocation and line items showing detailed budget administrative costs and operations costs for the financial year 2014/2015.[95]

Item codes	Line items	Proposed budget estimates (optimal level)	Proposed allocation based on mtef[95]	Variance (funding gap)
A	**Wage**			
211104	Statutory salaries	6 434 813	5 838 048	596 766
Subtotal		**6 434 813**	**5 838 048**	**596 766**
B	**Non-wage**			
211103	Allowances	1 238 697	1 101 040	137 657
212101	Social security contributions (NSSF)	740 261	671 288	68 974
212201	Social security contributions (gratuity)	1 751 299	1 581 659	169 640
213001	Medical expenses (to employee)	2 539	2 539	–
213002	Death and funeral expenses	13 462	6 539	6 923
221001	Advertising and public relations	13 842	9 310	4 532
221002	Workshops and seminars	–	–	–
221003	Staff training	3 011	2 942	69
221004	Recruitment expenses	3 077	–	3 077
221006	Committee, council and board expenses	46 708	46 708	–
221007	Books, periodicals, and newspapers	54 906	44 140	10 766
221008	Computer supplies and IT services	65 538	37 427	28 111
221009	Welfare and entertainment	58 454	58 034	419
221010	Special meals and drinks	4 915	4 915	–
221011	Printing, stationery, photo and binding	59 093	41 315	17 778
221012	Small office equipment	4 333	1 308	3 025

95 This table does not indicate results for the required 3–5 year period, for which information was not available. See Mulyagonja I 'Budget framework paper and medium term expenditure for the fiscal year 2014-2015 to 2016-2017 presentation to legal and parliamentary affairs committee'. Available at: *http://www.igg.go.ug/updates/news/ IG-presents-budget-framework-paper-and-medium-term-expenditure-framework-for-the-fy-201415-201617/*[accessed: 20 June 2014]. The figures are indicated in US dollars at a rate of USD 1=UGX 2 600.

96 MTEF refers to the medium-term expenditure framework. It provides an ex-ante framework to align resources with program priorities. See Devan D L (2001) The budget and medium-term expenditure framework in Uganda. *Africa Region Working Paper Series No. 24 (1)*. Washington, DC: World Bank.

Item codes	Line items	Proposed budget estimates (optimal level)	Proposed allocation based on mtef[95]	Variance (funding gap)
221014	Bank charges	–	–	–
221017	Subscriptions	20 502	20 502	–
222001	Telecommunications	148 077	148 077	–
222002	Postage and courier	5 169	5 169	–
222003	Information communication technology	26 455	26 455	–
223001	Property expenses	539	539	–
223003	Rent-produced assets	718 028	718 028	–
223004	Guard and security services	8 962	8 962	–
223005	Electricity	43 385	43 385	–
223006	Water expenses	5 908	5 908	–
223007	Other utilities	960	960	–
224002	General supplies of goods and services			–
224003	Classified expenditure (information fund)	55 846	55 846	–
225001	Consultancy services (short term)	5 769	5 769	–
227001	Domestic travel	1 424 256	913 905	510 351
227002	International travel	78 219	59 194	19 025
227004	Fuel, lubricants and oils	226 868	164 326	62 541
228001	Maintenance (civil)	17 700	16 496	1 404
228002	Maintenance (vehicles)	150 078	104 493	45 585
228003	Maintenance (machinery, equipment and furniture)	29 662	14 716	14 946
262201	Contribution to international organisation	15 385	15 385	–
263104	Grants to central ministries (PAF)	–	–	–
282101	Donations	4 323	4 323	–
415001	Trade creditors	–	–	–
Subtotal		7 046 422	5 956 985	1 104 822
Total (wage + non-wage)		13 481 236	11 779 647	1 701 588

Item codes	Line items	Proposed budget estimates (optimal level)	Proposed allocation based on mtef[95]	Variance (funding gap)
C	Development: Government of Uganda			
211103	Allowances	76 923	76 923	–
227001	Domestic travel	82 098	82 098	–
227004	Fuel, lubricants and oils	38 462	38 462	–
228002	Maintenance (vehicles)	19 231	19 231	–
231004	Transport (equipment)	273 077	273 077	–
231005	Machinery and equipment	48 846	48 846	–
231006	Furniture and fixtures	11 785	11 785	–
311101	Land	576 923	576 923	–
312206	Gross taxes	250 000	250 000	–
Sub-Total		1 377 344	1 377 344	–
D	Development: Danida			
221001	Advertising and public relations (radio and TV)	44 231	44 231	–
221002	Workshops and seminar A-C week & ex. prog.	57 327	57 327	–
221003	Staff training	94 707	94 707	–
221011	Printing, stationery, etc.	16 924	16 924	·
222007	Telephones and other utilities	15 854	15 854	–
227001	Travel inland (investigations and prosecution)	401 322	401 322	–
312201	Machinery, furniture and vehicles	57 692	57 692	–
312202	Computers, fax Machine, filing Cabinets	54 636	54 636	–
Subtotal		742 692	742 692	–

Relationship with the public and other stakeholders

The inspectorate has mechanisms in place to engage with the judiciary, parliament and the executive. With regard to the judiciary, several matters that are prosecuted by the IG's office are heard before a specialised anti-corruption division of the high court. The inspectorate also collaborates with parliament in various ways. However, the highlight of this relationship is the work of the Public Accounts Committee (PAC) of parliament, which complements the mandate of the IG in fighting corruption. The PAC, in 2012, detected various irregularities in the management of public funds in the prime minister's office and directed the inspectorate to investigate further, and to prosecute the responsible parties. With regard to the executive, the IG advises the executive on various matters, especially those involving abuse of office and corruption.

The inspectorate maintains a healthy relationship with civil society and the media. For example, as mentioned above, the IGG signed an MoU with the Uganda Debt Network to implement the SACM activity of the transparency, accountability and anti-corruption component of the NUSAF II. In terms of the MoU, the Uganda Debt Network is working with the inspectorate to build the capacity of communities to monitor government-funded projects in order to enhance transparency and accountability. In May 2014, community monitors and regional managers from various community monitoring groups were trained in anti-corruption reporting mechanisms. In the same spirit, the inspectorate and the media enjoy a cordial relationship, which has resulted in media coverage of the activities of the inspectorate and in media reports on abuse of office and corruption. As mentioned above, the media reported on corruption and abuse of office in relation to the Uganda National Roads Authority contract to construct the Mukono-Katosi road, a contract that was irregularly awarded to a non-existent entity. At the time of writing, the matter is being investigated by the inspectorate.

The inspectorate does not have prominent relationships with private-sector organisations beyond those mentioned above. This may be attributed to the fact that the IG is interested in corruption and abuse of office in public bodies. This mandate is constraining, especially in cases where corrupt acts involve public officers conniving with private-sector actors.

The inspectorate works closely with development partners. Denmark has been very active in supporting the work of the IG in combating corruption in Uganda. In 2012, when Denmark suspended aid as a result of corruption scandals in the Office of the Prime Minister, support for the inspectorate was not affected. Similarly, the inspectorate works closely with other countries' national agencies having a similar mandate. The current IGG, Irene Mulyagonja, is the outgoing chairperson of the East African Association of Anti-Corruption Authorities (EAAACA). Uganda's membership of the EAAACA has yet to provide substantive benefits. However, the EAAACA is being used to conduct joint training of staff from the member associations and has also encouraged information sharing to combat corruption. Uganda is also a member of the Eastern and Southern Africa Anti-Money Laundering Group (ESAAMLG). Membership of the ESAAMLG is resulting in substantial gains in eliminating corruption. The 2013 Anti-Money Laundering Act was enacted and is being implemented. The financial intelligence authority which is charged with implementing the act is now being set up. Sydney Asubo, the former director of legal services in the inspectorate is the interim executive director.

As discussed previously, the Constitution of the Republic of Uganda enjoins the inspectorate to report to parliament at least biannually on its performance and functions. These reports are discussed by parliament and can be an indirect platform for objective public perception of the inspectorate's mandate and activities.

Finally, the activities of the inspectorate are decentralised. This has helped investigations and monitoring at the local-government level. The Constitution and the Inspectorate of Governance Act provide for the establishment of branch offices at district and other administrative levels.

Reporting mechanism and public perception

The inspectorate is not under any duty to report findings of its investigations to the public. Information arising from these inquiries is treated as privileged information and is protected by law. Section 23 of the Inspectorate of Government Act provides that proceedings of inspectorate investigations are to be treated as if the investigations were proceedings in a court of law. This privilege is subject to laws that permit disclosure of such information, such as section 17(2) of the 2008 National Audit Act, which provides for the auditing of accounts of public entities, and section 5 of the 2005 Access to Information Act, which provides for the right to request information held by government or a public body. The latter law has yet to bear fruit, as requests for information and subsequent litigation have largely been unsuccessful. For example, in *Charles Mwanguhya Mpagi and Izama Angelo vs. Attorney General* (Miscellaneous Case No. 751 of 2009), a request for information on petroleum production sharing agreements (PSAs) signed by the government was denied. A number of similar requests have been denied, and, to date, the government has not released information on PSAs. Outside the petroleum sector, a number of citizen requests for information brought under the ATI law continue to be refused. This may be attributed to government officials being ignorant of the requirements of the law, as well as fear of political persecution in cases where the information may be perceived to be anti-government. The ATI law therefore remains largely unimplemented and citizens have, for the most part, had to seek recourse in courts of law, with considerable success.

H. The IG's performance

The reasons for the establishment of the inspectorate can be disaggregated into political issues and governance consolidation. With regard to the political narrative, the government sought to create a system that would nip corruption in the bud by exercising an oversight mandate over the conduct of government officials. It is worth noting that point seven of the ten-point programme, which was the governance vision of the National Resistance Army/ Movement (NRA/M), was the elimination of corruption and abuse of power.[97] In 1998, the Inspectorate of Government Statute was enacted.[98] At this time, the then young NRA/M

---

97   See A Ruzindana (1997) 'The importance of leadership in fighting corruption in Uganda.' In: KA Elliot (ed.) Corruption and the Global Economy. Washington, DC: Institute for International Economics. Available at: http://www. petersoninstitute.org/publications/chapters_preview/12/7iie2334.pdf [accessed: 11 July 2014].

98   Literature indicates that the IGG's office was established in 1986, but the Act was only passed in 1988. See M Martini (2013) Uganda: Overview of Corruption and Anti-Corruption. U4 Anti-Corruption Resource Centre, CMI, Bergen, Norway [U4 Expert Answer 379].

government was seeking to build credibility, especially within the international community. For example, in the same period, the Uganda Truth Commission was established. It has been argued that this was part of the broader strategy to cleanse Uganda's image abroad.[99] This reason, though superseded by the Constitution, continues to play an important role, especially in harnessing credibility with development partners and the broader international community. After 1995, the Constitution (chapter 13) was enacted and, subsequently, the 2002 Inspectorate of Government Act was passed into law. These pieces of legislation were mainly enacted to consolidate the governance structure and the position of the IGG established under the earlier Inspectorate of Government Statute.

The IG has been successful in creating an environment that reduces corruption. The mere existence of the IG's office discourages corruption, at least in the lower echelons of the public service. A considerable number of public servants are afraid of the negative press reports and of the prosecutions that come with corruption. That said, the IG has, in large part, been unsuccessful in instilling fear among senior civil servants and members of the cabinet.[100] This is also reflected in its prosecution strategy, which appears to focus on junior- or mid-level civil servants. The support of the head of government can at best be described as ambivalent.[101] It also appears that the government has used the IG's office to achieve political interests.[102] This has been the problem with some investigations involving political figures, such as Uganda's former vice president, Gilbert Bukenya, whose case is discussed below.

Table 4.2: Cases prosecuted by the IG

Uganda vs. Prof. Gilbert Bukenya CR.SC	Uganda vs. Geoffrey Kazinda HCT-00-SC-0138-2012
Formerly vice president of Uganda and MP.	Formerly principal accountant in the Ministry of Finance serving in the Office of the Prime Minister.
It was alleged that, between 2006 and 2007, and while chairing the Commonwealth Heads of Government Meeting (CHOGM) cabinet subcommittee, Bukenya directed the awarding of a contract for the supply of 80 BMW vehicles and outrider motorcycles to Motorcare Uganda Limited in total disregard of procurement procedures.	Kazinda diverted project money for his own benefit. This case is only one of a litany of cases. For example, Kazinda currently stands accused before the anti-corruption court of diverting public funds for personal gain by misappropriating nearly USD7 692 307 (equivalent to about UGX20 billion).
In a sudden turn of events, the president announced that he had been advised that Bukenya was innocent. Subsequently, the IG withdrew all charges.	Kazinda was convicted of abuse of office, among other charges, and is currently serving a term in prison.

99 See United States Institute of Peace (n.d.) Truth Commission: Uganda 86. Available at: http://www.usip.org /publications/truth-commission-uganda-86 [accessed: 11 July 2014].
100 K Allard. Lowenstein International Human Rights Clinic, Yale Law School and Human Rights Watch (2013) 'Letting the Big Fish swim': Failures to prosecute high-level corruption in Uganda.
101 Ibid.
102 Ibid.

It is important to further highlight the performance of the IG through analysing cases that have been investigated and prosecuted by the IG. The methodology adopted for this analysis is a review of one successful prosecution and another that was unsuccessful. In this regard, success is measured in terms of securing a conviction. Of course, this standard may not necessarily portray the performance of the IG. However, given the fact that prosecution is highly influenced by political interference, securing a conviction is an acceptable measure of good performance. The cases highlighted clearly indicate the approach taken when the accused persons have political influence as opposed to cases when the accused are merely junior- or mid-level civil servants.

The cases demonstrate the approach of government to cases involving high-ranking political figures. The decisions of the courts in both cases are in the public domain. In the case of Bukenya, the charges were dropped. In the case of Kazinda (a mid-level civil servant), several cases are ongoing. It is too early to determine the outcome of them all, though, as indicated above, Kazinda was convicted of abuse of office and sentenced.

Table 4.3: Complaints and matters handled from July to December 2013[103]

Complaints	Agency	Investigated	Agency	Tried	Agency	Convictions	Agency
1 513	IG	254	Police/IG	82	IG	3	IG/Court

I. Conclusion

Corruption in Uganda remains a significant challenge. The elimination of corruption was one of the pledges that featured prominently on the ruling NRM's agenda before it came to power in 1986. Indeed, true to its promise, the new government embarked on a process of setting up structures to fight corruption by, among others means, enacting a law that established the office of the IG. This spirit of setting up structures to fight corruption was maintained during the constitution-making process of 1995 and eventually the enactment of the 2002 Inspectorate of Government Act. In addition to this, a number of anti-corruption laws have been passed over the last 19 years. For the most part, these criminalise corruption and other related offences. Others establish a number of safeguards against corruption, such as asset declaration, access to information, and the protection of whistle-blowers. These furthermore promote accountability and enable a corruption-free environment. Enforcement of these laws is vested in a number of institutions, including the IG, the DPP, the Office of the Auditor General, and the Leadership Code Tribunal, which is yet to be appointed. In 2009, a separate court was set up to try corruption and related offences in a

---

103 The timeline for handling complaints is not available. We are in the process of obtaining the average time taken. These figures are computed from figures and tables in the IG's report to parliament for the period July to December 2013. See IGG Inspectorate of Government Report to Parliament July–December 2013. Available at: http://www.igg.go.ug/static/files/publications/IGG_REPORT_DEC_2013_2.pdf [accessed: 11 July 2014].

bid to streamline the prosecution of corruption-related offences and bypass case backlogs in the mainstream judiciary

The above steps are some of the most important in the fight against corruption, and, on the face of it, Uganda has one of the best anti-corruption systems in the region. The dilemma, then, remains the fact that the country is still ranked among the most corrupt in the region. This study has established that this mismatch is largely the result of utter lack of political will to end corruption by the leadership. The absence of political will has manifested itself in a number of ways, including interference with the work of anti-corruption institutions, selective prosecution, poor funding of anti-corruption initiatives and institutions like the IGG, failure to constitute a Leadership Code Tribunal, and the protracted delays in the appointment of a substantive IGG and DIG. The inspectorate was only fully constituted 18 years after its establishment. These acts and omissions greatly frustrate the effective investigation and punishment of the corrupt.

For this reason, a significant number of Ugandans have lost hope in the law and have learnt to accept corruption as a way of life. This is especially true where those implicated are politically well connected to the ruling regime. Although a number of these individuals have been charged and tried, there has only been one conviction, and that involved a former state minister for health. Even then, his conviction was quashed on appeal. The president is known to have come out openly and undertaken to cover all costs of the appeal.

It is this prevailing situation that has encouraged the growing tides of corruption in the country. Over the last five years, the country has witnessed a significant increase in cases of grand corruption involving theft and huge losses of public funds. According to the World Bank, the country loses an estimated USD300 million to corruption every year.[104] Political corruption and patronage are equally rampant.

Corruption greatly restricts the delivery of public goods and services, especially to those who cannot ordinarily afford these services. The culture of rampant corruption and perpetuated impunity serves as a recipe for civil strife and political unrest. It is therefore important that graft, and misappropriation and mismanagement of public funds are decisively confronted. This will take the complete reinstatement of political will, urgent legislative reforms and strict enforcement of the newly enacted laws that combat corruption.

---

104 See: http://www.aprm-au.org/admin/pdfFiles/Progress_Report_No1-Uganda_NPoA_30-06-2009_EN.pdf.

J. Recommendations

In order to address some of these challenges, the report makes the following recommendations:

1. Strengthen the overall legal framework for combating corruption

- Uganda has ratified the AU Convention. It should therefore enact the prescribed articles of the continental convention.
- The recently proposed amendments to the 2009 Anti-Corruption Act that provide for mandatory confiscation of property of persons convicted of corruption and related offences should be urgently and expeditiously adopted and enacted.
- The offence of causing financial loss and that of abuse of office should be clearly and specifically defined in line with international and regional norms and standards. The current definitions are overly broad and vague, which makes it difficult for the prosecution to sustain charges related to the two offences.
- The present scope of officers to which the code under the Leadership Code Act applies should be extended to include presidential appointees.
- The proposed Non-Governmental Organisations (NGO) Act (Amendment Bill), which imposes a number of stringent restrictions on mobilisation and interactions with communities by NGOs, should be dispensed with in order to create an enabling environment for NGOs to promote awareness of corruption.
- Investigative and prosecutorial roles of the IGG and DPP should be streamlined under the law to avoid the present overlaps and the duplication of the already constrained resources.
- Parliament should expeditiously put in place a legal framework for establishing a Leadership Code Tribunal, as prescribed under chapter 14 of the Constitution, so as to enable the full implementation of the Leadership Code of Conduct.

2. Strengthen agency status (legal framework, appointment, tenure and removal procedures, external oversight, autonomy and independence)

- The Leadership Code Tribunal should be constituted as a matter of urgency. In particular, parliament should embrace its constitutional mandate and by law establish the composition, jurisdiction and functions of this tribunal in the enforcement of the Leadership Code Act.
- The tenure of the IGG should be extended beyond the current four years to a non-renewable term of at least seven years. This will enhance the IGG's security of tenure and boost the independence of the inspectorate as a whole.

3. Strengthen the mandate and interagency collaboration of the IG with state and non-state actors, and with regional/continental networks

- The office of the IG and the attendant legal framework do not encourage interaction between the IG and the private sector. This, in many ways, constrains the work of the IG. It is important that the legal framework and the mandate of the IG be expanded so that this inspectorate can undertake investigations in the private sector when it is suspected that government officials have illegally influenced certain decisions, or that public funds have been illegally invested in private entities.
- The ongoing reform of the police and the judiciary should be enhanced and expedited if the work of the inspectorate is to be effective. As long as these institutions remain weak or ridden with corruption, the IG will be severely limited in its capacity to successfully bring officials implicated in corrupt practices to book.
- The role of the Public Accounts Committee of parliament should be supported, since it complements the role of the inspectorate. This may be done through strengthening the capacity of members by way of relevant training.

4. Improve agency financing, independence and sustainability

There is a need for the executive to demonstrate its commitment to fighting corruption. This can only be done if the IG is provided with sufficient financial resources. The current insufficient budget allocation is an indication of the executive's perception of the role of the IG. It is possible that the IG is only considered to be a means of averting donor fears and is not intended to actively tackle corruption. It is important that the funding variance of about USD1 701 538 is provided in order for the IG to function effectively.

5. Strengthen administration, staff capacity and infrastructure

The remuneration of the staff of the IG should be increased so as to reduce their vulnerability to manipulation and bribery. Although it is difficult to arrive at specific figures in this respect, one way of achieving equitable remuneration might be through a comprehensive review of the salaries of all public servants by a salaries commission established for the purpose.

The IG has, until recently, focused on the prosecution of low- and mid-level civil servants. This prosecution strategy directly protects high-ranking civil servants and those with political clout. It is important that the IG treat all cases equally and expeditiously. This may be difficult considering Uganda's political reality. Securing the tenure of the IG and other officers in the entity may give the IG more independence to prosecute all public servants regardless of seniority, status or influence.

Printed in the United States
By Bookmasters